Their Terrifying

Vernon Coleman

Books by Vernon Coleman include:

Medical
The Medicine Men
Paper Doctors
Everything You Want To Know About Ageing
The Home Pharmacy
Aspirin or Ambulance
Face Values
Stress and Your Stomach
A Guide to Child Health
Guilt
The Good Medicine Guide
An A to Z of Women's Problems
Bodypower
Bodysense
Taking Care of Your Skin
Life without Tranquillisers
High Blood Pressure
Diabetes
Arthritis
Eczema and Dermatitis
The Story of Medicine
Natural Pain Control
Mindpower
Addicts and Addictions
Dr Vernon Coleman's Guide to Alternative Medicine
Stress Management Techniques
Overcoming Stress
The Health Scandal
The 20 Minute Health Check
Sex for Everyone
Mind over Body
Eat Green Lose Weight
Why Doctors Do More Harm Than Good
The Drugs Myth

Complete Guide to Sex
How to Conquer Backache
How to Conquer Pain
Betrayal of Trust
Know Your Drugs
Food for Thought
The Traditional Home Doctor
Relief from IBS
The Parent's Handbook
Men in Bras, Panties and Dresses
Power over Cancer
How to Conquer Arthritis
How to Stop Your Doctor Killing You
Superbody
Stomach Problems – Relief at Last
How to Overcome Guilt
How to Live Longer
Coleman's Laws
Millions of Alzheimer Patients Have Been Misdiagnosed
Climbing Trees at 112
Is Your Health Written in the Stars?
The Kick-Ass A–Z for over 60s
Briefs Encounter
The Benzos Story
Dementia Myth
Waiting

Psychology/Sociology
Stress Control
How to Overcome Toxic Stress
Know Yourself (1988)
Stress and Relaxation
People Watching
Spiritpower
Toxic Stress
I Hope Your Penis Shrivels Up
Oral Sex: Bad Taste and Hard To Swallow
Other People's Problems

The 100 Sexiest, Craziest, Most Outrageous Agony Column
Questions (and Answers) Of All Time
How to Relax and Overcome Stress
Too Sexy To Print
Psychiatry
Are You Living With a Psychopath?

Politics and General
England Our England
Rogue Nation
Confronting the Global Bully
Saving England
Why Everything Is Going To Get Worse Before It Gets Better
The Truth They Won't Tell You...About The EU
Living In a Fascist Country
How to Protect & Preserve Your Freedom, Identity & Privacy
Oil Apocalypse
Gordon is a Moron
The OFPIS File
What Happens Next?
Bloodless Revolution
2020
Stuffed
The Shocking History of the EU
Coming Apocalypse
Covid-19: The Greatest Hoax in History
Old Man in a Chair
Endgame
Proof that Masks do more harm than Good
Covid-19: The Fraud Continues
Covid-19: Exposing the Lies
Social Credit: Nightmare on Your Street
NHS: What's wrong and how to put it right
They want your money and your life.

Diaries and Autobiographies
Diary of a Disgruntled Man
Just another Bloody Year

Bugger off and Leave Me Alone
Return of the Disgruntled Man
Life on the Edge
The Game's Afoot
Tickety Tonk
Memories 1
Memories 2
Memories 3
My Favourite Books

Animals
Why Animal Experiments Must Stop
Fighting For Animals
Alice and Other Friends
Animal Rights – Human Wrongs
Animal Experiments – Simple Truths

General Non Fiction
How to Publish Your Own Book
How to Make Money While Watching TV
Strange but True
Daily Inspirations
Why Is Public Hair Curly
People Push Bottles Up Peaceniks
Secrets of Paris
Moneypower
101 Things I Have Learned
100 Greatest Englishmen and Englishwomen
Cheese Rolling, Shin Kicking and Ugly Tattoos
One Thing after Another

Novels (General)
Mrs Caldicot's Cabbage War
Mrs Caldicot's Knickerbocker Glory
Mrs Caldicot's Oyster Parade
Mrs Caldicot's Turkish Delight
Deadline
Second Chance

Tunnel
Mr Henry Mulligan
The Truth Kills
Revolt
My Secret Years with Elvis
Balancing the Books
Doctor in Paris
Stories with a Twist in the Tale (short stories)
Dr Bullock's Annals
The Awakening of Dr Amelia Leighton

The Young Country Doctor Series
Bilbury Chronicles
Bilbury Grange
Bilbury Revels
Bilbury Country
Bilbury Village
Bilbury Pie (short stories)
Bilbury Pudding (short stories)
Bilbury Tonic
Bilbury Relish
Bilbury Mixture
Bilbury Delights
Bilbury Joys
Bilbury Tales
Bilbury Days
Bilbury Memories

Novels (Sport)
Thomas Winsden's Cricketing Almanack
Diary of a Cricket Lover
The Village Cricket Tour
The Man Who Inherited a Golf Course
Around the Wicket
Too Many Clubs and Not Enough Balls

Cat books
Alice's Diary

Alice's Adventures
We Love Cats
Cats Own Annual
The Secret Lives of Cats
Cat Basket
The Cataholics' Handbook
Cat Fables
Cat Tales
Catoons from Catland

As Edward Vernon
Practice Makes Perfect
Practise What You Preach
Getting Into Practice
Aphrodisiacs – An Owner's Manual
The Complete Guide to Life

Written with Donna Antoinette Coleman
How to Conquer Health Problems between Ages 50 & 120
Health Secrets Doctors Share With Their Families
Animal Miscellany
England's Glory
Wisdom of Animals

Dedicated to Antoinette

Thank you for being you and for being with me.
Thank you for every day you spend with me. Every day
is a gift from God.

`Over that little life that still remains to me,
and at my death, deign that your hand be present:
You know You are the only hope I have.'
(From the Canzoniere by Petrarch)

Their Terrifying Plan

Vernon Coleman

Contents

Part One

1

It is customary, when writing a book explaining how and why something has happened, to put the history bits first; to explain the past before dealing with the present and, possibly, the future.

In this book I have done the opposite.

I have begun, in Part One, with an account of the world in which we live, drawing attention to the anomalies and inconsistences, the threats and dangers and so on. It is an objective analysis of the world in which we live, and the anomalies and apparent coincidences which now make up our everyday lives.

In Part Three, I have analysed the events which have brought us to this unhappy state; the very brink of the Great Reset and the New World Order. In this part of the book I have explained in some detail the who, the why, the what, the when and the how. Many apparently unconnected events have taken us slowly but certainly towards the position we are in now: on the very brink of the Great Reset and a permanent loss of our freedom and the essentials of our humanity.

It can be confusing and bewildering to try to work out why a bunch of billionaire bankers should stand behind gangs of communists, neoliberals and rampant fascists. The attraction of fascists for communists, and vice versa, is no mystery. They appear to stand, or sit, at the far ends of a political continuum but in fact the continuum is a circle not a line and fascism and communism sit closely together. The term 'neoliberal' is, of course, merely an acceptable, modern replacement for the word 'communist'. But why would billionaire bankers sit with neoliberals?

The explanation is a simple one.

The billionaire bankers know that a world government will mean that someone has to look after all the finance, commerce and natural resources and take control of all the money. And they, the bankers, will selflessly step forward to take control – with the neoliberals providing the front men and women for a totalitarian government which appears to rule the world but which merely serves as an administration for the puppet masters. A world government will

1

mean a world court, a world army, a world central bank with a single (digital) currency, a world tax system, a world welfare state, world economic planning, mandatory population control of some kind and with health and education organised on a global scale. It will also mean that members of the public will not be allowed to own any weapons. Think about it carefully and you will realise that some of these aspects of world government already exist and the rest are in preparation.

A look at Part Three of this book will show you precisely how the bankers and financiers have, throughout the 20th and 21st century, already succeeded in using politicians and organisations such as the United Nations to enable them to take control of many of the world's resources, much of the world's wealth and, indeed, whole countries. This part of the book is a timeline for the accumulation of oppression, deceit and egregious corporate and institutional behaviour. The billionaires and bankers have for decades been investing billions of dollars in their takeover and they have been using taxpayers' money, and the hard work of small farmers and workers everywhere, to help them take control. They have used defence spending and foreign aid programmes to enable them to take more and more power, and they have financed social unrest and the absurd climate change myth in order to introduce legislation which furthers their ambitions and gives them ever more power over everyone and everything. In a fair and decent world power should be shared among the people. In the world which the globalists are preparing, all the power will be in the hands of a few, unelected, greedy, self-centred individuals.

I haven't filled this book with references because to do so would add a month to the time taken to prepare the book for publication. And there isn't time. Time is running out. Also, to do so would double the size and price of the book. Readers who question or doubt any of my assertions can easily check their validity by doing research of their own (remembering, of course, that the essence of good research is to know what questions to ask and where to look to find honest answers – usually outside anything associated with mainstream media organisations, which have persistently and determinedly refused to print evidence which does not support the theories which are favoured by the conspirators).

It is vital to understand that there is no evidence that man-made climate change is a dangerous threat, or even exists, and a considerable amount of evidence to show that changes in the weather are nothing more than the ordinary climactic changes which have occurred since man first started noticing and recording the weather. The sometimes scary scenarios publicised by the climate change cultists (for whom the collective term should be 'enemies of mankind') are nothing more than scaremongering propaganda produced by people who will never allow any debate or discussion about their prognostications. It is important to remember that for some years now the conspirators, desperate to create changes in the weather, have dumped millions of tons of potentially toxic sun-blocking nano-particulates such as alumina, barium and strontium above the earth in sometimes successful attempts to affect the weather, damage crops and cause mass starvation. And as their efforts begin to work, they will demand more restrictions and more lockdowns and claim, inevitably, that these are necessary because of the changes in the weather which will by then have taken place.

Remember, everything I have reported in this book can be easily checked from reliable sources. I have included a short bibliography at the end of this book to help you do your own research. I own and have read all these books (and many more) in preparing this volume.

2

The conspirators are winning (and they obviously are) because they have taken complete control of the mainstream media and much of the internet. They know that if you control what people read, see and hear then you can control what they think. The mainstream media has always been fairly corrupt but in recent years the corruption has become absolute. Broadcasting organisations such as the BBC and newspapers such as *The New York Times* now specialise in the dissemination of propaganda, misinformation and disinformation, rather than news.

Propaganda used to be crude. It used to consist of posters and slogans and it used to be promoted in a pretty obvious sort of way. Simple, dramatic propaganda probably reached its apogee during the First World War when the English were taught that the Germans were eating babies. In Germany posters everywhere simply read 'God Punish England'.

But slowly, the psychologists and the brain washing experts took over and propaganda became infinitely more subtle and ever-present.

In 1957, Vance Packard wrote a book about advertising and he called it *The Hidden Persuaders*. He explained how advertising copywriters used psychological tricks to persuade us to buy the products they were selling. They sold soaps and deodorants by suggesting that if you didn't use their product then, well, not even your best friends would tell you the unpleasant truth. Copywriters used guilt, greed and envy to make consumers open their wallets and their purses and to spend more than they could afford on products they didn't really need but had been tricked into believing that they wanted or had to have.

Today, most propaganda is unrecognisable as such. Crude threats of pestilence, war, famine and death have been replaced with subtler, created fears. Occasionally a triptych phrase or an advertisement will stand out as rather obvious and clumsy but most of the time ideas and fears are promoted and 'sold' in the same way as cars or cornflakes but are sold with a subtlety which makes it nigh on impossible for the casual observer to realise that they are being manipulated. And, of course, that isn't surprising since the people behind the manipulation are well-qualified professionals, many of them trained in war-time psychological techniques used to oppress and convince resistant civilian populations.

Propaganda isn't always what it seems to be and even intelligent observers can sometimes find it difficult to work out precisely what the ultimate aim of a particular campaign might be. Some propaganda material appears on official government advertisements, of course, but most of it appears in the traditional mainstream media. As the pandemic fraud began in 2020, so shops and businesses began to stop buying advertising. There was no point in companies spending money on buying adverts when all the shops and most places of business were closed by the strict lockdowns that were in force around the world. (The key thing to remember is that everything that happened at that time happened in virtually every country in the world. Never before had such strict and identical laws been introduced on a global scale.) And so governments stepped in with huge advertisements, bought every day at full price. The big mainstream media companies (newspapers, magazines, radio and television) had never had things so good. Internet companies also found that they were receiving huge amounts of advertising money from governments. And, of course, in the UK the BBC had already been bought with the licence fee and the huge hand-outs of taxpayers' money which the corporation had become accustomed to receiving.

(In addition, the BBC entered into a financial arrangement with a certain Bill Gates, an amateur vaccine enthusiast and professional investor in vaccine companies, whose enthusiasm for hiring doctors and nurses to stick needles into strangers was and is unprecedented. It is difficult to think of a more disreputable organisation. Gates, like Prince Andrew, was a close friend of Epstein and has financial links with many media companies including *The Guardian* which published a painfully obsequious article about him. The BBC has broadcast lies, denied truths, taken sides, when it is supposed to be impartial, supported the EU, from which it has received bucket-loads of money, and broken at least one very significant promise – to provide free TV licences to those over 75.)

And to make sure that propaganda works most effectively, the people paying for the propaganda ensure that their messages remain free of opposition by using censorship to control critics and those offering questions or alternative points of view.

Propaganda and censorship are twin, synergistic weapons used to control public opinion and to promote the views (whatever they may be) of those paying for the propaganda and the censorship. Opinions and facts which don't fit the conspirators' agenda are suppressed or completely banned.

(It has recently been suggested, by a social psychologist, that students should be taught how to counter conspiracy theories and propaganda. Such a scheme was introduced in Finnish schools in 2014. I would welcome such a scheme if I had any faith that those teaching the curriculum were able to define 'propaganda' fairly and objectively. Sadly, the evidence shows that the world is awash with dishonest, bought-and-paid-for fact checkers and 'misinformation and disinformation' units (such as the one run by the BBC) which merely promote and defend what the conspirators tell them to promote and defend.)

The result of all the propaganda, is that most people still seem to think that the barrage of bad things happening are all happening now by accident or by coincidence. That simply isn't true. Everything is happening on purpose; everything is orchestrated. There is a malign force manipulating our lives – a malign force controlled by the conspirators. It is no accident that there is now an untreated global epidemic of anxiety and depression with mental health problems now probably the commonest health disorder affecting children. It is terrifying to see that in the UK well over eight million people are being actively treated with anti-depressant drugs (which, for the record, have been shown not to work).

Today, propaganda is used to manipulate and to control.

All things considered it is perhaps not surprising that there are so many strikes around the world, why violent riots are commonplace, why inflation is soaring, why health care is deteriorating rapidly, why travel has become deeply unpleasant (when it's possible), why millions of children are illiterate and innumerate, why the police no longer bother investigating serious crimes and why corruption is now so commonplace that no one in authority notices or cares.

3

While propaganda around the world has been spread by professional teams of misinformation specialists, debate and balanced discussion has been banned.

For years now it has been illegal even to discuss the holocaust (which was, uniquely, dignified with an initial capital letter, in the same way that covid was subsequently given an initial capital letter or, in many cases, written out entirely in capital letters to make the word look even more important).

I don't question the holocaust. I don't pretend to know what happened or did not happen.

What I do find immensely troubling is that experts who claim to have evidence, or substantiated views, can be sent to jail simply for wanting to debate the accepted truth.

And this clampdown on debate is being extended.

The mainstream media refuses to debate climate change, the covid pandemic or the dangers of vaccination – among other things. A very dangerous precedent has been set. Governments want

6

criticism of vaccination programmes to be treated as terrorism. At least one US Presidential candidate for the 2024 elections has said that critics of climate change theory should be put in prison.

Since the 1980s, the climate change myth has been promoted with great certainty by the controlled mainstream media. But nothing that has happened in the last century has been in any way abnormal, and for cultists and meteorologists to claim that they are able to warn with confidence of what the weather will be like in 50 or a 100 years time is extraordinarily nonsensical, since weather forecasters have a job to predict what tomorrow's weather will be like with any degree of accuracy.

The truth is that the majority of climate change scientists do not agree that man-made climate change is a problem and most of the hysterical warnings which have appeared in the media have been based on computer simulations and are worthless.

For a brief summary of the climate change fraud I recommend a small book entitled 'Greta's Homework', written by Zina Cohen. Many of the most absurd scaremongers have been proved wrong time and time again. So, for example, one leading expert (Dr Kenneth E.F.Watt, an ecologist at the University of California, predicted that the world would be 11 degrees colder by the year 2000 and that we would be in an Ice Age.)

There is no scientific evidence supporting the politically motivated claim that climate change is a real problem. The climate change myth was created by the globalists who are desperately trying to create a threat which will move us towards a world government. And sadly, now, most people don't question what they are told. Some are too frightened of what they might hear to ask questions; they don't want to know the answers and they don't want to have to confront the fact that they are living in a world where the propagandists (such as the *New York Times*, the *Washington Post* and the BBC) have turned black into white and white into black. Some simply do not believe that they could have been lied to so consistently and so vehemently.

The same is true of other scare stories which have been run in recent years. Broadcasters, newspapers and respectable sounding pressure groups have all lied constantly and consistently about the ozone layer, acid rain, pollution and infections.

Huge amounts of money are being made by the campaigners and professional agitators who run the organisations and charities trying to 'sell' the myth of climate change.

As happened with AIDS in the latter part of the 20th century, anyone promoting the officially approved party-line will be swamped with grants and financial support.

(I remember debating the issue of AIDS on LBC radio in London. Afterwards, standing on the pavement outside the studio, I asked my 'opponent', a campaigner for a homosexual group, if he really believed the nonsense he had shared with the audience. He readily admitted that he didn't, but that he had lied and produced fake figures simply to try to win the argument. He was, he said, concerned that if AIDS were considered to be a problem which only affected homosexuals then it would receive no public support or money.)

On the other hand, anyone who questions the myth will be destroyed professionally. Television performers who stick to the globalists' line about climate change are feted and offered vast sums of money while those who even dare to question the official line suddenly become unfashionable and unemployable.

Those who argue that man-made climate change is a serious problem consistently refuse to debate their views in public. As with the covid-19 vaccine, the refusal to debate is good evidence of a fraud and a cover up.

The result of all the lies is, I'm pleased to report, that the majority of people simply don't believe that climate change is real. Even after being bombarded with threats and fears, managed and controlled by governments, pressure groups and international bodies such as the United Nations, most people remain resolutely sceptical.

4

The true story of the conspiracy taking us towards the Great Reset and the New Normal is a story of unprecedented wickedness.

It is a story which has taken me years to unravel. It is a story of deceit, corruption and of a small group of men and women with an unquenchable thirst for power and an unnatural appetite for wealth. It is a shocking story which explains how a small group of relentless megalomaniacs have manipulated billions of people around the world into believing a completely fabricated myth – the myth of man-made climate change – solely so that they can take complete control and create a new world government. (Note: the term 'climate change' is now frequently used together with the prefix 'existential' as though this gives this entirely unsubstantiated theory some gravitas.) It is a story of how well-meaning but naïve individuals have been tricked into believing carefully concocted lies about the environment, and then acting as if those lies were true. It is a story of financiers and billionaires bribing and pulling the strings of politicians and bureaucrats. It is a story of endless deceits. It is a story of conspirators deliberately turning free men and women into slaves, unable to take responsibility for their own actions and totally dependent upon the State for everything they do. It is a story of ruthless advocates for fake pandemics deliberately creating fear and panic and then offering some sort of solution. This is, in short, a story of the most horrifying, evil plot ever concocted by man and in this book I will give you the evidence showing how this fraud has been carefully and deliberately manufactured.

Throughout the world, governments have accepted the agenda force-fed to them by a cadre of neo-liberals. Exactly the same economic rules are now applied everywhere. So-called reforms introduced by the World Bank, the International Monetary Fund (IMF) the World Trade Organisation and the Federal Reserve, and the central banks under the auspices of the Bank of International Settlements in Switzerland, and all sponsored by the Bretton Woods institutions have created a perfect environment for global banks and multinational corporations. The label 'neoliberal' might imply a kindly, free market system but under the authority of the neoliberals a new system has been created which gives authority, power and pretty well nearly all the money to the bankers. As both Plato and Aristotle recognised, wealth is addictive. The bankers behind the conspiracy to create a World Government can never have enough money. They manipulate, they lie, they cheat, they defraud and they have no feeling for the people from whom they steal. As long as they get another billion or two in the bank they don't care about the millions who die. And they prefer to make their money without having to work for it.

5

I should mention, in passing, that the IMF and the World Bank and so on are regulatory bodies which were created to operate on behalf of the world's governments but in practice they operate on behalf of the world's biggest banks and corporations and work with secretive and unelected organisations such as the Trilateral Commission, the Bilderbergers, the Council on Foreign Relations the International Chamber of Commerce, the Trans-Atlantic Business Dialogue, the United States Council for International Business, the Institute of International Finance and the World Economic Forum. It is the last of these, the WEF, with its annual meetings in Davos, which is perhaps the most dangerous. (I will explain how these organisations work in Part II of this book.) These organisations meet in secret with bankers and do so in closed sessions. Most of their deliberations and conclusions are secret – even though the costs of their meetings, and the huge costs of the security provided may be met by taxpayers.

6

You have been subjected to a barrage of lies for much if not all of your life. You have been the victim of a confidence trick of brobdingnagian proportions; a deceit that even the Baron Munchausen would probably find too unlikely.

And yet, as I have promised, everything I'm about to tell you is true. In Part Three of this book I have named names and places and I've given dates in order to explain precisely how, when, where and why this fraud has been systematically concocted. The globalists describe anyone who questions what is happening as a 'conspiracy theorist' but when you've read Part Three, you will realise that this conspiracy is no theory.

The bottom line, the unavoidable, unpleasant truth, is that everything is far worse than you thought it was. The world is not being deranged by accidents; it is not being derailed by coincidences. Everything that is happening has been carefully planned; everything is deliberate. We are victims, you and I, of the biggest, longest and most comprehensive conspiracy in history. Slowly, methodically and ruthlessly, a relatively small group of conspirators have steadily taken control of every major institution in the world. They have bullied world leaders, they have replaced kings and presidents with their own men and they have stolen and deceived in a way that the Cosa Nostra would surely envy. The conspirators are for the most part American and phrases such as 'US exceptionalism' and the 'reserve currency dollar' mean that the United States can ignore international law, tell other countries what to do, invade sovereign states with impunity, wage wars at someone else's expense, build up massive, international debts which they never intend to pay off, steal natural resources (such as oil, gold and minerals) without compensation or apology and force countries to hand over assets and local monopolies to multinational companies in America.

All around the world billions of people have been threatened, impoverished, bullied and punished in order to enrich American banks, American financiers and American corporations. In many cases where Americans have invaded and stolen resources they have left behind chaos and abject poverty. Look, for example, at what happened to Iraq, Libya and Syria to give but three modern examples.

And the final irony is that despite the fact that it has pillaged and raped whole continents, the United States is now by far the world's largest debtor. It has successfully turned the dollar into a way to make other countries finance its global war mongering. The foreign reserves of central banks around the world consist of dollar dominated assets and only now (in 2023) are countries such as China, India and South Africa demanding new principles for international law, trade and finance.

(It is curious, by the way, that millions who believe in the existence of the Cosa Nostra find it impossible to believe that well-educated men and women from good families could possibly be involved in an even bigger scheme to control the world's population. The members of the Cosa Nostra, the Triad and similar organisations are content with running drugs and prostitutes, and to protect their enterprises they steal, maim and kill hundreds of people. The conspirators, the bankers and financiers, and their allies (whom I classify as the collaborators) want control of everything and everyone and to protect their ambitions they steal, maim and kill hundreds of millions.)

And both conspirators and collaborators have acquired a robust sense of entitlement.

A medium level bureaucrat working for the Government in India accidentally dropped his smart phone into a reservoir. So he had the reservoir drained, with millions of gallons of water being wasted, so that he could look for his phone.

Everywhere in the world, on an hourly basis, entitled bureaucrats abuse their power in a thousand different ways.

7

The wickedness, the limitless greed, the hypocrisy, the blatant cruelty, the ruthlessness and the depravity of American politicians, bankers and billionaire financiers is hard to believe.

For over a century ruthless men and women, some of them well-known, some of them the holders or former holders of public office, some of them secretive and anonymous and some of them freelance power brokers who have moved effortlessly from the world of finance to the world of government and back again. So, for example, numerous executives have moved between banks such as Goldman Sachs on the one side, and governments and the most powerful NGOs (such as the World Bank and the International Monetary Fund) on the other.

Rents, interest and huge financial charges (including massive bonuses paid to bankers whether or not they have done their jobs well) are, bizarrely, counted as 'financial services' and listed in a nation's accounts as part of the country's Gross Domestic Product.

(Financial services should really be regarded as debts and countries, such as the United Kingdom, where financial services make up a major part of the nation's GDP must inevitably be doomed. In those countries, real productivity (making things and providing genuine services) have become secondary to the provision of lending money and the fees and charges associated with moneylending.)

Anyone who questions the role of the banks is, inevitably, described as a 'conspiracy theorist' and as 'discredited'. Those terms appear time and time again; so often that it is clear that they are designed and spread by specialists working for agencies such as the CIA. And the abuse is decorated with decades old stories which can be rewritten to produce doubt, by manipulated truths, by half-truths and by downright lies. Anyone who questions governments and

12

bankers will be labelled a conspiracy theorist and called discredited by a fake encyclopaedia called Wikipedia which appears to be controlled by the CIA and similar organisations from other countries.

(Larry Sanger, the despairing co-founder of the site Wikipedia, has used the word 'corrupt' to describe his creation. A deal between Wikipedia and Google means that the lies put on Wikipedia are reproduced on Google to reach a larger audience.)

The lies help to prevent anyone exposing the conspiracy from reaching more people. The conspirators and the collaborators who work for and with them are specialists in psychological warfare and in the basic elements of 'controlled opposition'.

The key thing to remember is that there are now no coincidences in geopolitics or modern history and nothing is happening by accident. However chaotic and unpredictable and out of control you feel things are, you should understand that everything that has happened in the last few decades (and particularly in the last three years) was planned. It was, indeed, planned so carefully and with such precision that for the last three years in particular, since early 2020, it has been possible to forecast what will come next. (I have predicted almost everything that happened since early 2020 and the evidence for that is available on my websites.)

I naturally hope that as many people as possible will read the evidence I've collected and will ignore the attempts by the conspirators and the collaborators to discredit me and the book. Sadly, most of the people who should read this book won't touch it; they won't read it because they have been brainwashed by the mainstream media working for the conspirators.

8

I have been thoroughly discredited and demonised by the establishment, and the fact that for over 50 years I have produced accurate predictions and analyses has been suppressed and ignored. The very fact that this book will not be available in bookshops or public libraries, and will not be reviewed, or even mentioned in the mainstream media, tells us much. My books have been published by many leading hardback and paperback publishers and have been translated into 26 languages and sold around the world. But, as with my other books on this subject, I will have to publish this book myself because no orthodox mainstream publisher will dare publish it. In the past most of my books were serialised in newspapers and magazines. Several of them were turned into series for television and radio. This book will not appear anywhere else. Like everyone else telling the truth I am lied about, sneered at and ridiculed by agents working for the conspirators. I no longer care that saying this makes me sound paranoid because I know that I am not.

The conspirators were never going to take any chances. They knew that once they had begun their campaign towards the Great Reset (formerly known as the Great Merger) their propaganda campaign would be opposed by people who could see through the lies and the misinformation.

And so, right from the start, they knew that they would have to stamp down hard on anyone (especially doctors or media professionals) who dared to question the official line. Anyone who didn't agree wholeheartedly with the idea of the Great Reset was demonised as a right wing extremist and immediately discredited.

Branches of the military and the secret services were employed to attack and discredit the truth-tellers. In the United States of America the CIA has been extremely active in this area. And the FBI has worked with Ukrainian intelligence to censor and suppress Americans on social media (in breach of their first amendment rights). In the UK, much of the work of disinformation, misinformation and demonization and abuse has been in the hands of the British Army's 77th Brigade. For example, right from the start the 77th Brigade put abusive and libellous remarks in the comments section underneath videos questioning the official line on the pandemic. The abuse was often crude. My videos were constantly full of libellous comments claiming that I did not have a medical degree, that I was a fake and a fraud. And GCHQ (the UK Government's spy centre and eavesdropping agency) was ordered 'to wage cyber war on anti-vaccine propaganda' and 'to take out anti-vaxxers online and on social media'. GCHQ, paid for by British taxpayers, has used dirty trick tactics to control, infiltrate, manipulate and distort online information. GCHQ's own Twitter account claims that their 'brightest people bring together intelligence and technology to keep Britain safe' but in May 2021, the European Court of Human Rights ruled that GCHQ's methods violated the right to privacy and that its regime for the collection of data was unlawful. Who at GCHQ decided that the agency had the right to suppress the truth and to promote lies is still a mystery. The end result of this treachery has been that thousands of people have been killed or injured because they were denied information about the covid-19 'vaccine' which might have helped save them from listening to inaccurate information on the BBC and other areas of the mainstream media.

A slightly more subtle approach was to hire individuals to pretend to be on the side of the truth-tellers. I suspect that at least half of those claiming to be 'truth-tellers' were actually working for the opposition. Some have ridiculously complex organisations and they have often been hugely successful at collecting money. (Some have collected millions of pounds from gullible supporters and, in some cases, big fees from drug companies.) And there were others who regarded the pandemic as a career booster and were pliable enough to be allowed onto mainstream television and radio stations where what they said could be directed or manipulated. (The real truth-tellers were not allowed access to any mainstream media.)

There is nothing new in any of this, of course. The authorities have always infiltrated pressure groups or those who threaten to cause disruption.

I have always been very active in the campaign against animal experimentation and back in the 1970s and 1980s anti-vivisection campaigns were regarded as the major terrorism threat in the UK. The security services, MI5 and Special Branch, admitted that the absence of outside, traditional terrorists meant that in order to justify their existence they had to find some alternative and anti-vivisection groups were selected as the most suitable target. This sometimes had bizarre consequences. On one occasion a group of five alleged extremists was arrested. Unfortunately, it was quickly found that four of the alleged extremists were actually representatives of various official groups. One was a member of Special Branch, one was an MI5 officer, one was a policeman and one was an undercover journalist. Only one member of the group was a bona fide animal rights activist. Initially, the activist was charged with the very serious offence of conspiracy but the case quickly fell apart, and was abandoned, when the prosecutors realised that a conspiracy requires two or more individuals – you cannot change a solitary individual with conspiracy. This was not an isolated instance. It was common

15

place to find that groups protesting or campaigning against animal experimentation had been infiltrated by those promoting or supporting vivisection – though the majority of the infiltrators were being paid, either by the Government or by the drug industry.

Much the same thing is happening today among those telling the truth about the banks, climate change, fake pandemics and toxic 'vaccines'.

9

There is much bewilderment among intelligent doctors and scientists as to why so many doctors kept quiet about the lies being told when the covid-19 hoax and the fake pandemic unfolded. Around the world, hundreds of thousands of doctors kept quiet about the covid-19 'vaccine' and continued to prescribe a product which has been accurately described as the most dangerous and damaging single pharmaceutical product ever marketed. The covid-19 jab did not do what the establishment promised it would do but, at the same time, it caused countless thousands of deaths and serious injuries among the patients who were injected.

There are two explanations for the fact that so many doctors ignored the evidence and did what they were told to do by dishonest advisors within the medical establishment and bought and paid for journalists and celebrities.

The first explanation is that all over the world doctors were extraordinarily well paid to give the covid-19 jabs. Hospitals were given bribes (labelled as bonuses) which were dependent upon the number of patients they injected. Doctors were bought off, and dissuaded from asking too many questions, by being paid well over the normal fees for giving vaccinations. Those doctors will, in due course, appear in court where they will be unable to mount any sort of defence. To say that they behaved unprofessionally and greedily is a massive understatement.

The second explanation is that doctors were too terrified to speak out against the medical establishment because they saw what had happened to colleagues who dared to share their views with their colleagues and the general public and who had had their licences removed by the official licensing authorities and, in addition, been vilified by the media .

The truth, so well hidden during the last three years, is that the medical establishment was, as it has been for decades, controlled by the pharmaceutical industry and instead of looking at the facts licensing authorities around the world merely did as they were told to do. Numerous doctors lost their licences, and their livelihoods, because they dared to speak out and tell the truth. The majority of doctors, seeing what had happened to those who spoke out, kept quiet and betrayed their patients, themselves and their profession. Those gutless wimps should be ashamed.

In the United Kingdom, doctors are licensed by the General Medical Council, an organisation which is, in theory at least, a charity but which appears to have some of the worst qualities of a quango, a government department and an enforcer for the drug industry. I believe that drug companies control governments, they control the medical establishment and, it appears, they may also control the UK's medical licensing authority – the General Medical Council.

The GMC has become infamous for its extraordinarily one-sided defence of the exaggerated covid pandemic and the pointless but enormously dangerous covid vaccine.

When the fake pandemic was first promoted in February and March 2020, I immediately described the covid scare a hoax. The figures available proved without any question that the danger of what was clearly merely a rebranded annual flu had been massively exaggerated by people who had a bad track record at assessing the relevant figures. In the UK, the Government's own official advisors agreed with me, dismissing the covid-19 infection as being no more dangerous than the annual flu. Inevitably, perhaps, their expert advice appears to have been ignored in favour of advice from a mathematician with a terrible track record.

Naturally, the conspirators behind the exaggerated risk did not like my description of the covid scare as a hoax (a video I made was seen by many millions within days) and I was quickly demonised and lied about in the media. The GMC couldn't take away my licence because their own administrative rules meant that, as with many doctors, my retirement from active practise meant that I'd had to give up my licence. But younger doctors, who were convinced by my arguments or who reached the same conclusions, were to feel the full wrath of the drug company controlled medical establishment.

17

So, for example, consider the case of Dr Mohammad Adil who, until three years ago was a respected surgeon working in the NHS. Three years ago, Dr Adil criticised the Government line on covid, and the GMC responded by taking away his licence – meaning that he could no longer practise as a surgeon or, as a doctor in any capacity. Three years later, Dr Adil still didn't have his licence back. The cost to him has been extraordinary. And we should not forget the cost to the NHS. If we consider that in those three years he could have performed 1,000 operations a year – not an unlikely number – then his three year banishment means that 3,000 patients have been denied the operations they needed.

Several other doctors in the UK had their licences removed for criticising the absurd and indefensible covid policy. And exactly the same thing happened around the world where licensing authorities have ignored the scientific evidence and punished doctors who dared to share the truth with the world – usually on social media.

It was this unscientific bullying, and the widespread publicity given to the consequences, which ensured that thousands of doctors kept quiet – frightened that they too would lose their licences and their livelihoods. A doctor without a licence to practice is as useless as a sweep without his brushes or a taxi driver without a cab.

The GMC's decision to deny Dr Adil his licence was always unjustifiable.

First, there is the question of free speech. Article 19 of the United Nations Charter states clearly that 'everyone has the right to freedom of opinion and expression'. There is no codicil limiting the rights of doctors. The GMC's decision is in direct opposition to this fundamental human right. It has been argued that doctors have a special responsibility because of their position and training but this strengthens rather than weakens the UN charter. Doctors have a special responsibility to speak out when they believe that something is wrong. And, of course, you can't have a little bit of free speech any more than a woman can be a bit pregnant. You either have free speech or you don't. To say that a doctor cannot criticise the medical establishment is as nonsensical as saying that an opposition party politician cannot criticise the Government. The licensing authorities which have removed doctors' licences for speaking out are undeniably in breach of the UN Charter. How a lawyer or a judge can justify allowing any licensing body to deny an individual's right to protection from the UN Charter is, I confess, a mystery to me. Doctors are entitled to share their views with the public and the public is entitled to decide whom to believe.

Right from the start the doctors supporting the Government and drug companies have steadfastly refused to debate in public, and the mainstream media has taken an entirely biased, unbalanced one-sided line in reporting the fake pandemic. The BBC, ignoring its own charter and repeated claims of fairness, has even stated that they would not interview anyone questioning the value of vaccination whether they were 'right or wrong'. I have frequently challenged vaccine supporters to a live, national public debate. None has had the confidence or the courage to accept the challenge.

(The conspirators and the collaborators have not just refused to debate the pros and cons of the covid vaccine. They have refused to debate any of the contentious issues. You might think that the most confident conspirators and collaborators would be delighted to have the opportunity to debate their beliefs about climate change, the Great Reset and their plans for a world government, and to air the details of the science which they claim is behind their new religion. But they don't want to debate and the only logical conclusion is that they know that they would lose any debates because they have no supporting evidence.)

Second, the GMC has assumed that the Government and the medical establishment must always be correct and beyond criticism. This is dangerous nonsense. One doesn't have to go very far back in history to find numerous examples of times when the Government and the medical establishment have been completely wrong and, as a result, patients have suffered until doctors had the courage to stand up for the truth. When Dr John Snow gave chloroform to Queen Victoria, there was an uproar in the medical establishment because it was felt that women should not be given anaesthesia during childbirth. Electroconvulsive therapy, leucotomies and the removal of vast lengths of the intestine were all approved by the medical establishment but later condemned. It was because of the medical establishment that tonsils were removed without good reason. No one knows how many children died as a result. A good deal of unnecessary heart surgery has been performed on patients because of bad medical practices promoted by the medical establishment. It was because of bad medical practices condoned or encouraged by the

19

medical establishment that millions of patients became hooked on barbiturates and then benzodiazepines. And I wonder how many of those who have condemned Dr Adil know that widely used and previously approved vaccination programmes have been condemned as worthless and dangerous.

History shows that the medical establishment has been wrong more often than it has been right, and if the GMC stops doctors criticising the Government and the medical establishment (known to be linked to the pharmaceutical industry) then nothing will ever change for the better.

If we go back a little further in medical history we come across individuals such as Dr Semmelweiss whose work on women lying in labour wards changed medical practice and saved thousands if not millions of lives. Dr Semmelweiss was, of course, viciously attacked by the medical establishment. There are many more examples in my book 'Medical Heretics'.

The undeniable truth is that history shows that the medical establishment has always suppressed the truth and promoted profitable lies. Nothing has changed. The medical establishment still promotes medical procedures which don't work, while suppressing essential but inconvenient truths. The GMC's fundamental mistake appears to me to be that it has assumed that its loyalty should be to the medical establishment rather than to the welfare of patients.

Third, and more directly perhaps, the evidence now shows quite clearly that the medical establishment's official line on covid-19 was completely false. Everything that the establishment has said and done has been wrong and dangerous. The General Medical Council and all those who supported its decisions seemed to have assumed that the establishment was right.

If they had looked closely at the evidence they would have known that the UK Government's own scientific advisers decided, back in March 2020, that covid was not a major threat. They would have known that Government statistics show that the number of people who died from covid-19 was no greater than the number who die from flu every year (a disease which had mysteriously and conveniently disappeared). Indeed, the number of deaths from what was clearly a rebranded flu was no greater in 2020 and 2021 than it was in some previous years. Moreover, it is now clear that the absurd policies of lockdowns, social distancing and mask wearing were without any scientific foundation, were unnecessary and dangerous and were in part responsible for the entirely predictable increase in deaths which marked 2022 and will continue for some years to come. The PCR test was never intended to be used as it was, and has been proven, beyond any doubt, to be of no more value than a coin toss. It is clear that the closing down of schools and businesses was also entirely unnecessary and has done massive, long-lasting damage. Worse still, it is now abundantly clear, and generally accepted by intelligent, well-informed doctors and scientists, that the covid-19 vaccine was never properly tested, was never fit for purpose and is the most dangerous and deadly pharmaceutical product ever marketed. Largely because of links with the pharmaceutical companies involved, the Government and the medical establishment misled the public and the health professions. All the evidence for these claims is available on my website and books and in over 300 videos I made between the years 2020 and 2023. (The videos first appeared on YouTube but they were removed piecemeal pretty well as soon as they appeared. And then my entire channel was removed for the new crime of telling truth.)

Finally, there is one other rather shocking reason why the GMC should not have made any rulings about Dr Adil or any other doctors who criticised the official line on covid-19 and the covid-19 vaccine.

The General Medical Council (in my view one of two big enemies of patients in the UK – the other is the British Medical Association) has invested nearly £1,000,000 in fast food and drink firms and, worse still, has invested large amounts of money from doctors' fees in drug companies. And one of the companies in which it had shares was one of the companies making a covid-19 vaccine.

How can the GMC judge doctors' behaviour in relation to covid and covid jabs when it has a vested interest in the financial success of vaccine manufacturers such as Astra Zeneca?

It could surely be argued that the GMC, which has money invested in vaccine manufacture, has a vested interest in protecting vaccine making and should not, therefore, discipline doctors whose actions might have damaged the earning potential of any companies in which it has invested its own money.

The GMC can be compared to a judge punishing someone for criticising a product in which he himself has a financial interest. Indeed, I would argue that the GMC, and its vast army of overpaid, and, it seems to me, sometimes arrogant, pen pushers has abandoned its role as a guardian of the public and become an enforcer for the pharmaceutical industry.

Those who had the courage to speak out should be applauded and it is they, not the promoters of a 'vaccine' that does not do what it was promised to do but which has caused many deaths and much illness, who should be honoured.

In a free and progressive society criticism of the establishment should never be subject to censorship.

My conclusion can only be that the General Medical Council is unfit for purpose and should be closed down immediately. It is not fit to hand out dog licences, and certainly not equipped to control the licensing of doctors. It has failed to do its job: to protect the public and it appears to me to have acted more in the interests of the pharmaceutical industry than the interests of patients.

I'm delighted to report that in July 2023, the British Medical Association agreed with my conclusion. The BMA's Annual Representative Meeting has passed a no confidence vote for the GMC and will now call for its leaders to be sacked.

The BMA motion said that 'too many' Medical Practitioners Tribunal Services fitness to practise decisions are 'disproportionate to the error of the doctors mistake' and expressed no confidence in the current tribunal.

Doctors voted for a motion calling for the leadership team of the GMC to be dismissed and replaced with a team that 'commands the confidence and support of the medical profession'.

10

It is a sad fact that most people are so indoctrinated that they have no interest in reading anything which may force them to question what their government (and government sponsored media) has told them to think.

The mainstream media has, of course, distracted millions with non-stories about celebrities, minor celebrities and members of the English royal family. The world is in a spiral of deliberately engineered destruction, and, with a designer war between NATO and Russia now well into a second year, it is well into World War III, but the mainstream media has pushed the war (and other terrible things which are happening) onto page seven or the end of the news. For the period of the war to date, it has concentrated its energies on the childish exhibitionism of a middle aged couple of former royals who seem to spend much of their lives making public announcements about their desperate desire to be private.

Despite this determined suppression of reality, there is still more than enough scary news around to keep people fearful. Recent large surveys have shown that most people now avoid all the news because they find it too depressing. They see no point in knowing about things which they feel they can do nothing about.

Meanwhile, individual governmental and international bodies use every small hazard as a reason to introduce new, comprehensive and suffocating legislation. A decade or two ago I suspected that this was no more than bureaucrats doing the only thing they know how to do – micromanage – but it is much more than that. The bureaucrats and rule makers have been encouraged to do everything they can to suppress the people.

Around the world, laws are being introduced to make it illegal to share information which is regarded by the Government as 'misinformation' or disinformation even though the news they share might be regarded by a majority of doctors and scientists as accurate. In Australia, for example, there is the Communications Legislation Amendment (Combatting Mis-information and Dis-information) Bill 2023 which will result in truth-tellers being fined up to $500,000.

There is no doubt that today a great many people are frightened to view the truth (or even something which they fear may be the truth) because the lies they have accepted have resulted in their doing things for which they would feel ashamed. So, for example, doctors and journalists who helped promote the wicked and fake covid fraud do not like to acknowledge the part they played in the creation of a false global panic. Nor do they like to see the evidence showing that the covid-19 'vaccine' which they recommended with such enthusiasm has caused many thousands of deaths and serious life-changing injuries.

Even if you know some of the truth this book will shock you. And it will perhaps surprise you to discover that the villains in the world are not the people whom we have been taught to see as villains (Putin, Xi, Gaddafi, etc.).

Our freedom is being taken from us at an incredible speed by people who appear to be respectable and part of the establishment. The ground work for the removal of our freedom was done decades ago. Now we are in the final stages of the takeover. It may sound insane but a small group of committed, self-serving extremists now dominate the political systems in all major Western countries and they control the global economy. It is because of this power and money hungry clique that we are controlled from birth until death by unseen hands. And the control is tightening by the day. The conspirators are introducing a digital world and a digital currency. There will soon be a global government, controlled by unelected but appointed individuals who, in turn, control our every move through the invidious system of social credit; a restrictive system which I described in some detail in my book *Social Credit: Nightmare on Your Street*.

11

The frightening thing about social credit, a sly, manipulative programme of control, is the way in which it is being introduced insidiously – without many people really noticing what is happening. For example, in England, the tax authorities will, in 2026, be introducing a new points system for those who pay their tax late. If a taxpayer collects a set number of points they will receive a financial penalty. On the roads, motorists have been told that if they bump into a cyclist they may be sent to prison for life. (Knocking over a pedestrian is fine, it seems, but cyclists must be protected.) And in school, children are being forced into a social credit system which even the Chinese might find horrifying. At a school in Devon, some pupils have been told that they cannot attend their school prom if they haven't accumulated enough 'praise points'. Pupils get 'praise points' in five categories: being ready to learn, enabling others to learn, treating the environment and others with respect, working to the best of their ability and fulfilling their responsibilities. 'Praise points' are apparently awarded by staff as a reward for 'positive behaviour'. One parent said: 'This has caused emotional harm and it is not kind and inclusive to these children banned from the prom'.

Of course it isn't. But I don't think anyone ever claimed that social credit schemes were designed to be kind and inclusive.

12

The conspirators are ruthless and heartless in a way which most of us find difficult to comprehend. They control everything we do. They control banking and transportation and health care and they already own or control most of the world's natural resources. They start wars, when wars suit their purposes (regardless of the death and destruction those wars will cause), they create hatred between black and white and between men and women and they push economies into recessions and depressions when to do so serves their purpose. The conspirators, who usually like to describe themselves as (and to be described as) 'philanthropists' deliberately introduce policies which they know will kill hundreds of millions of people, even billions of people, because they know that those policies will make them more powerful and ever richer. (The myth of philanthropy is commonplace among billionaires. John D Rockefeller Sr used to arrange for himself to be photographed giving dimes to children. This was the basis for his reputation as a philanthropist.)

The conspirators know that in order to continue to succeed they must convince the public that there is no conspiracy. And to do this it is vital, utterly vital, to suppress the truth and oppress anyone who dares to tell the truth. The mainstream media, bought and paid for, has enabled the conspirators to do this very effectively. Early in 2020 I began making videos for YouTube. I acquired a huge number of 'subscribers' within a couple of months and then my channel was entirely deleted and I was banned from making more videos or even accessing the channel. My crime was a simple but modern one: telling the truth. Facebook told me that I could not join their platform because I would be a danger to their community. (There was no discussion and no specific reason was given.) I was banned by all social media sites (though fake sites in my name appeared) and publishers suddenly refused to publish my work. Publishers around the world withdrew my books from sale – even when those books had been hugely successful. For example, publishers in China and Germany pulled all my books from sale because I had questioned the efficacy and safety of vaccination programmes. There was no debate, no discussion; publishers didn't ask me for evidence – my books were banished, to be pulped or burnt. Newspaper editors who had been enthusiastic about articles they wanted me to write suddenly stopped talking to me and wouldn't even say what had happened.

Censorship has long been a problem for authors, of course. *Animal Farm* by George Orwell was refused by a number of the publishers who saw it. One admitted that the Ministry of Information in London had advised him against publishing it.

And those doing the banning usually find some strange ways to excuse their actions. In June 2023, the European Union banned the publication of information which it thought did not support Ukraine with enough enthusiasm or which was regarded as supporting Russia in some way. Reporters who tried to put both sides of the story, and who attempted to tell the truth, were punished or fired. The EU claimed that it was controlling the flow of independent information and doing this to protect freedom of speech.

Journalists and commentators working for mainstream publishers are very well paid to ignore facts which might be inconvenient. In the US it has for some time been well known that the *New York Times* and the *Washington Post* are no longer fighting to publish independent truths; both seem too inclined to support the conspirators and the establishment. An American software billionaire, Bill Gates, a well-known lay proponent of the covid-19 vaccine, has given huge sums of money to *The Guardian* and to the BBC in England. *The Guardian*, for example, was given £12 million by Gates. The BBC, which had also received money from the European Union, had close financial links with the vaccine supporting billionaire. Both *The Guardian* and the BBC produced hagiographic profiles describing Gates as a philanthropist. Curiously, both organisations seemed subsequently to ignore Gates' links to Jeffrey Epstein, the disgraced financier. Other individuals, including an English prince and a leading bank executive, have been ruined by their connection to Epstein but, to the surprise of some, Gates remains relatively untouched.

As I have previously pointed out, at the height of the covid-19 fraud in 2020, one BBC presenter announced that the BBC would not debate the subject of vaccination with anyone criticising the vaccine 'whether they were right or wrong'. Such blatant prejudice is difficult to believe, particularly when offered by a State broadcaster which has a duty to provide a fair and honest assessment of the news. The only good thing you can say about the BBC staff is that they lie and promote propaganda with a straight face. When they repeatedly insist that two plus two equals five they do so with such solemnity that the mass of people believe them, and doubt their previous suspicion that two plus two comes to something else, a sum which they can no longer quite remember. The BBC has betrayed the licence fee payers, and obeyed the demands of its own left leaning liberal staff; promoting misinformation and disinformation with enthusiasm. During the fake pandemic in 2020, the BBC held meetings with the British Government and one can only assume that these meetings were to decide what lies to broadcast and what truths to suppress.

The art of spreading misinformation and disinformation successfully depends upon the victim being prepared to believe what he or she is told. Repetition of the misinformation is vital and it helps if those spreading the lies are regarded as reliable and honest. Over the years the BBC had built up a reputation as a respectable and honourable source of news but happily that reputation is now in tatters and surveys show that only a minority believe anything on BBC news programmes.

13

The pattern I have discovered, the map I've drawn, will not only explain what has already happened (not just in the last few years but going back longer than anyone alive can remember) but it will also enable you to see what we can expect in the future. We do not ordinarily see these things because they are hidden from us; they are disguised when they are not suppressed. Even when coincidences are pointed out to us we do not see them as connected because the lies are simply too great for us to comprehend ('no one could possibly do that', we say to ourselves) and the malefactors, the conspirators, too evil for us to understand. The conspirators who have driven the conspiracy forwards are not just bad men and women in the way we understand the word 'bad'. We tend to think of serial killers as evil but the evil of the globalists is far beyond anything most of us can comprehend. Obama, the Clintons, Blair, the Rothschilds, the Rockefellers et al are just as irredeemably evil as Attila the Hun, Genghis Khan, Stalin and other psychopaths. Their cold-blooded

27

manipulations are designed to destroy everything we hold dear and everything we respect as human. They live to manipulate by deceit. The conspirators are different to the rest of us.

Most people want to have some control of their own lives; they want a relationship, a home, some belongings and a position in their community. They want to do what they can to help others.

The conspirators are quite different: they want power over other people and they have an insatiable yearning for wealth. The conspirators' actions are driven by how they see their role in the world (not by any desire to help the world). American bankers see US hegemony and the dollar's position as the world's reserve currency as vital to their own wealth and so they will do everything to protect these things. They want a global government controlled by America. They want to create compliance, and slavery, through social credit. They use war to reduce a population which they regard as too large.

And who needs all those people when robots and artificial intelligence programmes can replace many of them? In spring 2023, two British telephone companies warned of massive redundancies with Vodafone announcing that it was sacking 11% of its workforce and British Telecom expecting to sack 42% of its work force. Most of those made redundant will never work again and their skills will be allowed to wither. Supermarkets are sacking staff members and replacing them with automated tills. Soon the shelves will be stocked by robots. Banks are closing branches and pushing their customers to do all their banking online.

One of the aims of Artificial Intelligence programmes is to make demoted humans feel worthless, insignificant and powerless. The manipulators are using the myth of climate change to create naïve followers who do their work for them in destroying ordinary society.

14

Through a potent, toxic mixture of greed and selfishness, the neoliberals are deliberately destroying mankind in order to enrich and empower themselves. (The neoliberals really came into power with Bill Clinton's Democratic Party in the US and with Tony Blair's Labour Party in the UK.)

If they succeed with their plans for the Great Reset, everything we are and care about will die, not inevitably, as the stars are dying, but murdered by the evil few (far, far fewer than nought point one per-cent of the population), and their complacent, complaisant collaborators who do everything they are told to do to oppress and suppress and who probably make up between one and five per cent of the population.

I suspect that many of the collaborators, confused, ignorant, uninformed, unimaginative, greedy, obedient and paid well beyond their natural skills, do believe what they are told; they believe that the world is threatened by man-made global warming and that there really was a dangerous epidemic in 2020.

Back in 2020, I warned that the collaborators would be our nemesis. I still stand by that. Our main threat has always come not from the conspirators themselves, who are such a tiny number that they could not possibly have great influence over the world's billions, but from the politicians, doctors, central bankers, journalists, NGO officials and celebrities who defended the conspirator's theories and who promoted their wicked schemes; the lockdowns, the vaccines and their endless lies.

Electors everywhere keep putting their faith in political parties and in politicians. They vote for different parties in the everlasting hope that they will one day be served by an honest government. It has been said that one sign of lunacy is to keep doing the same thing in the hope that the outcome will be different. Every new government, everywhere in the world, promises much but delivers nothing. All political parties now make the same false promises and then ignore the will of the people who voted for them. Back in 1968, George Wallace pointed out that there wasn't 'a dime worth of difference between the two parties' in America. When voting is fiddled (as it is now in so-called developed countries, just as much as it is in undeveloped countries) it is not with the aim of putting a particular party into power but with the aim of establishing those individuals who are most readily controlled by the conspirators.

In what was perhaps a weak moment of honesty, President Franklin D Roosevelt, who was President of the United States between 1933 and 1945 (making him the longest serving President in American history) gave us a vital warning but I don't think anyone took him seriously and most people didn't listen. He said: 'In politics, nothing happens by accident. If it happens, you can bet it was planned that way.'

The fact is that things don't keep getting worse by accident, they keep getting worse by design.

Hopes and ambitions don't fade by chance, and it is no coincidence that everything seems to go wrong in every country in the world at the same time.

And anyone who draws attention to the evidence supporting these conclusions is regarded as deranged and is immediately discredited, abused and demonised. Professionals, experts in their field, who speak out against authority, are ostracised and usually dismissed as 'right wing extremists'.

You will have no doubt noticed that officially there are no left wing extremists but that everyone who questions what governments do will automatically be labelled a 'right wing extremist' or, worse still, labelled as a 'terrorist' or a 'fascist' or both. In practice, of course, right wing politicians have been moving steadily to the left for many years and today most leading politicians in the West are best described as neo-liberal. Since there is absolutely no ideological or technical difference between politicians on the very far left, known as communists, and politicians on the very far right, known as fascists, the neoliberals can themselves be accurately described either as international socialists, which is to say 'communists' or as 'national socialists', which is to say 'fascists' or 'neo-Nazis', according to how you feel.

In reality, the political spectrum should have totalitarianism at one end and anarchy at the other. All modern political parties are, however, best described as totalitarian in method and intent since their aim is to take total control over aspect of our lives. There is no difference between communism as defined by Marx, total control as defined by the Illuminati in the 18th century and the Great Reset (the New Normal) as proposed by the World Economic Forum, the United Nations and all main political parties around the world.

When politicians, bankers and billionaires around the world all get together to do the same things in order to take control of the world's population, what else can you possibly call it other than a 'conspiracy'?

(Those who are puzzled by what is happening, ask why well-known billionaire financiers could possibly advocate communism.

The answer, of course, is that under the sort of communism practised in the USSR and China, the people at the top of the pile lived very different lives to the lives endured by the masses at the bottom of the pile. Today's billionaires may publicly advocate a very left wing brand of socialism but in fact they manage to protect their wealth and to avoid paying taxes by having their money, their super yachts, their private islands, and their mansions in the middle of huge acreages, carefully protected in trusts and foundations. Socialism and communism are promoted because they are the most efficient way to control the wealth and activities of the ordinary citizens. Communism may be promoted as a way to give power to the people but in practice the plan is to transfer all power to a bunch of greedy megalomaniacs.)

Eventually even those who want to speak out are frightened to do so because they see what happens to their colleagues. And the ignorant, half-blind collaborators who have done the demonising and the sneering find that they are in a position where they cannot speak out even if they eventually do see the truth. They are committed to the lies they've told because to tell the truth would expose their lies. (And, in the case of doctors, for example, expose them to massive lawsuits.)

Our daily enemies have for years been the woke citizens who have, for the most part unknowingly, served as helpers for the conspirators who have been working against us for a century or more, and who are now coming out into the open a little more as their battle to create a New World Order reaches its zenith. (For the record the phrase 'New World Order' was adopted for the title of a book by H.G.Wells in the 1940s but the phrase was also used by Richard Nixon in the early 1970s. Nixon used the phrase frequently and it was regarded as referring to a world super-state – or the world government which has been the aim of the conspirators for decades.)

Encouraged by the conspirators (who are experienced at using the naïve and slightly simple-minded to promote their cause) the woke collaborators have done their best to destroy our histories and our culture. They have torn down statues and worked hard to damage the reputations of those who opposed the conspirators. So, for example, the woke collaborators frequently target Winston Churchill, attacking his statue and his books. Anyone who has ever stood up for freedom in any way is maligned and must be erased from culture and history.

15

Justice and liberty are now little more than historical concepts; illusions which are today only believed by the naïve, the gullible and, of course, the completely compliant. Judges are as corrupt as politicians, journalists and doctors and everyone in public life.

Western societies were set up to separate the various parts of government, and we are taught to believe that is how things still are. Thomas Hobbes said that 'freedom is government divided into small fragments'. But it isn't how things are today. The various branches of government, the parts dealing with the making of laws, the administration of laws, the control of the police, finance, banking and the trade unions may appear to be separate but in practice they have been brought together. Nothing shows this more clearly than the way the European Union operates. The European Parliament has virtually no powers and all the decisions are taken by unelected eurocrats who are themselves controlled and influenced not by citizens but by lobbyistst. When the English people voted to take their country out of the European Union in the historic 'Brexit' vote, the establishment (which is to say the highly paid civil servants and others employed in various ways to administer Government policies) simply refused to make any real changes to the way the country is run. The result was that a barrage of new laws were passed by the English Parliament and added to the thousands of EU laws which should have been abolished, but which were kept.

As Lord Acton famously said: 'Power tends to corrupt and absolute power corrupts absolutely.'

Government money (which is to say taxpayers' money) is regularly used to reward favours and to buy complicity and silence. And, as the population struggles with roaring inflation, interest rates higher than many people could remember (or were prepared for), disruption caused by climate change nutters, threats of this and that from governments, quangos and the mainstream media, the unions have introduced massive pay demands designed, it seems, to create rifts and to make the poor ever poorer. Doctors demanded a 35% pay rise and when that was refused, went on strike and increased their demand to 45%. Hospital consultants threatened to go on strike and they too wanted a 35% pay rise to add to their minimum £120,000 a year. Nurses went on strike. The poor and the elderly were left behind. Most demands came from state employees (who were already the best paid and the least hard working and had the best perks such as pensions and the ability to work from home or not at all when the fancy took them).

Who was behind the endless strikes?

The usual culprits of course.

The globalists behind the strikers knew that civilisations collapse when the gulf between rich and poor gets too big and that is exactly what is happening. And, of course, the middle classes are being destroyed with ever increasing taxes.

Individual liberty and free speech have been sacrificed for what we are told is the collective good.

We live in totalitarian states where we are no longer expected to think for ourselves or to manage our own lives in the way we see fit. How long will it be before we are not allowed to think at all?

16

The two party state has become the one world state.

It is impossible to discern any real difference between the two main political parties in the US or the two main parties in England. All parties support the war against Russia, all supported the covid fraud. The parties pretend to squabble occasionally but it is all play fighting. We are now inches away from a World Government and since the (American owned) International Monetary Fund has already established its first global tax agreement, the World Government isn't far away.

Fifty years ago we were told that the world's socialist governments would come together, under the auspices of the United Nations, to form a global super-state. (China was brought into the United Nations because the conspirators knew that in order to control all the world's banking and resources, they needed every country in the world to join the UN.) This new coalition would, it was said, be the Great Merger. Nothing much has changed except that things are now moving much rapidly towards global governance and the joining together under what has been mysteriously renamed the Great Reset.

It is interesting to note that back in 1950, Richard Nixon, who was a congressman at the time, introduced a 'resolution calling for the establishment of a United Nations police force'.

And so it came about, of course.

But the United Nations didn't limit itself to a police force. Psychologists, behavioural scientists, agronomists and others were employed to work out ways to control people.

Right at the beginning of the UN's life, there were plans to reduce the size of the world's population and to enforce sterilisation.

(It has been reported that some widely promoted vaccination programmes were actually designed to reduce fertility. Bill Gates, the amateur vaccine propagandist, claimed that the vaccines he was promoting would save lives and reduce the size of the population in Third World countries. It is difficult to see how those two opposing aims can be reconciled unless the vaccines being used had some effect on fertility – a possibility for which there is now a good deal of evidence. In numerous countries around the world, euthanasia programmes have been introduced in order to eliminate the elderly and the sick by encouraging them to end their lives. In 1953, Evelyn Waugh wrote a novel called *Love Among the Ruins* in which he described a state-run euthanasia centre. In Trudeau's Canada, the Government has introduced a very forceful euthanasia programme called 'medical assistance in dying'. There were 13,000 state sactioned 'suicides' in Canada in 2022, and that country is now deciding whether to allow children and the mentally ill to kill themselves. In the Netherlands, healthy individuals with autism are allowed the option of euthanasia, and Australia is deciding whether to let children as young as 14 kill themselves (or allow someone to do it for them). Today, euthanasia is legal in Belgium, Canada, Luxembourg, Netherlands, New Zealand, Spain, Columbia and parts of Australia.

In hospitals in the United Kingdom, it is now routine for patients who are admitted to hospital to ask if they want to be resuscitated if they fall seriously ill. Patients are warned that resuscitation can be painful and difficult and may leave them with broken ribs. As a result, many agree to have 'Do Not Resuscitate' labels put on their hospital charts. Patients who are frail or unable to give consent are often labelled 'Do Not Resuscitate' without the consent of relatives, and the decision not to provide care for patients who are seriously ill may be made by quite junior nurses instead of a team of doctors and nurses as used to be the case a few years ago.

17

All over the world, there are plans to destroy local police forces, to destroy local health care and education programmes and to make sure that all citizens (in countries such as the US) hand in their guns. The plans originated with the United Nations.

Anyone who has ever worked for the United Nations must have known exactly what was happening and must have understood the aims of the organisation for which they were working. UN staff are highly paid and lowly taxed, and were and are traitors who should be executed for their crimes against mankind.

18

To encourage citizens everywhere to accept the idea of more State control, it was decided that rioters should be allowed to disrupt towns and cities all over the world, ostensibly campaigning against racism, climate change and other issues. These plans were made over half a century ago. Individuals campaigning against the plan for a world government were silenced and arrested but individuals whose activities were considered 'acceptable' to the conspirators were allowed to do pretty much what they wanted to do. Today, there is evidence that the demonstrators who are left alone by the police (the ones campaigning for 'black lives' or for 'net zero') are receiving vast amounts of money from rich conspirators and, indeed, demonstrations are allowed only if they are approved by the conspirators. Groups of people complaining about the use of oil are allowed to disrupt traffic, damage buildings and cause massive inconvenience. In an attempt to appear even handed, the police will occasionally interfere and the courts will punish one or two of those involved but only well after the fact and never before – as frequently happens with those protesting about the conspiracy or about the monarchy. No one in Parliament seems to care overmuch that the activities of climate change protestors are undoubtedly responsible for far more deaths than climate change itself. People have missed essential hospital appointments, ambulances on emergency calls have been halted and motorists have been unreasonably subjected to the stress of interminable and unnecessary delays. The complicity of the police and the courts makes it clear that these illegal activities are condoned if not encouraged by the authorities. And as a bonus, the demonstrations provide excuses for the conspirators to introduce more oppressive laws, to give the police more powers and to take away freedom and privacy from everyone.

The campaigners don't realise it but they have been manipulated and controlled like so many puppets. Campaigns for affirmative action and positive discrimination and demands for reparation have been organised by the conspirators to create a new form of acceptable racism, designed to create anger and racial disharmony.

The acceleration of the climate change fraud which is promoted by a small but very vocal group of bad tempered, aggressive, hectoring and ignorant fools with no respect for others is taking us, unwillingly, towards the lunacy of net zero. The climate change fanatics (having feasted on a diet of pseudoscientific arguments) think they are now running the world. And, indeed, they are.

On the face of it, their hectoring and campaigning has been extraordinarily successful but in truth, of course, the campaigners have been allowed a free ride. The campaigners have been funded by bankers and billionaires who sometimes masquerade as philanthropists.

(All great fortunes were, of course, obtained through lying, cheating or stealing or all three and more. It is possible to become a millionaire through hard work and imagination but it is only possible to become a billionaire through dishonesty or through having an ancestor do something dishonest on your behalf).

The climate change fraud was, of course, all about money and power. The self-styled environmentalists and greens who promote the climate change myth want to stop African countries from using fossil fuels. Since without fossil fuels those countries will never be able to advance their civilisations in the way that countries in the West have progressed, it seems undeniable that the whole net zero climate change argument is irredeemably racist.

I'm afraid that environmentalists and Greens are often deeply unpleasant people. A fellow from New Mexico, called Dave Foreman, who co-founded an organisation called 'Earth First!' is reported to have described humans as 'a cancer on nature'. Foreman, an ultra-radical environmentalist, favoured 'demonstrations' in which members drove spikes into trees (potentially killing foresters and in at least one case resulting in the operator being severely injured), tore down power lines, sunk whaling ships and poured sand into the fuel tanks of logging equipment.

19

In 2020, the conspirators ramped up their battle to take over the world by introducing the entirely invented 'coronavirus pandemic hoax.

Right from the start it was clear that the pandemic hoax had been invented for three main reasons: to bring in some form of compulsory vaccination programme, to provide an excuse to exterminate a large number of old people (the conspirators have long felt that the world is overpopulated and long worried that the elderly population costs too much in pension payments) and to create a situation where cash could more easily be outlawed. That's what I said in February and March 2020.

There was more to it, of course.

The conspirators had decided to use their fake pandemic to help them lead the way forward to the development of a world government – the great reset, the new normal, the new world order.

All this was being promoted by the World Economic Forum (with its extraordinary enthusiasm for the abolition or private property, as promoted in the Communist Manifesto by Karl Marx) and by a secret organisation known as the Bilderbergers which consists of a bunch of bankers, arms dealers, drug company bosses, food company bosses and obedient politicians.

The fake pandemic with its lockdowns and enhanced compliance programmes was seen as an essential step towards the introduction of a system of social credit, digital currency and digital passports. The covid fraud was seen as a way to obtain total control over all citizens.

20

Central bankers, bankers and left wing politicians are all desperately keen to eradicate cash and to force everyone to use digital money –

in the form of credit cards, debit cards, crypto-currencies and accounts with organisations such as PayPal. Scores of central banks already have their digital currencies ready – eventually they'll be moulded into a single global currency known as the Universal Monetary Unit or, quite possibly, the Unicoin.

The standard argument of those who want to replace cash with digital currency is that using your smart phone at the till is more convenient than using cash. What the bankers and collaborators don't mention is that the price for that convenience is compliance and slavery. You can flash a piece of plastic, your watch, your smart phone or your tattooed or implanted wrist, instead of having to put up with the burden of carrying cash in a wallet or purse, but the unspoken downside is that in return you have to put all your trust in the integrity and good intentions of the bankers and central bankers – people who have already boasted that they will use your reliance on their services to decide how you spend your money, where you spend it and how much of it you are allowed to keep.

The bankers, the conspirators, want to control every transaction as part of the social credit-digital world they are building. Governments, banks, supermarkets, travel agencies, health care services, the police will combine their databases with YouTube, Google, Facebook and other monstrously intrusive organisations which collect, own and then sell your private information.

I've been warning about the end of cash for at least three decades, and the conspiratorial authorities have been pushing hard for the introduction of digital currencies since the days before laptops and smart phones.

Today, the bankers (aided and abetted by politicians) are closing banks as fast as they can (arguing falsely that everyone wants to bank online) and they're making it difficult to take cash out of your bank. ATM machines are rapidly disappearing, and if you try to take cash out of your account over the counter you could well end up being interrogated like a criminal.

Once the digital currencies become the only way to earn, save or spend, we will all be slaves. The central banks will be able to control our money. They already plan to limit each individual to between £10,000 and £20,000. Anything more than that will simply disappear. Negative interest rates will discourage savings. Money will have a limited shelf life – just as money in mobile phones can disappear after a few months. And the bankers will decide how you can spend your money.

It is worth pointing out, by the way, that the central banks have mostly become 'independent'. When this happened in the UK, in 1997 the Labour Government misled the country, saying said that it was giving the Bank of England its independence and granting it operational independence over monetary policy so that it could be free of government influence. In fact, this was rather dis-ingenuous since all central banks were modified to suit the requirements of the financial elites – who prefer to deal with independent banks. In the European Union, it was the Maastricht Treaty which gave independence to the central banks. The European Central Bank, in the EU is controlled by Deutsche Bank (which was for a long time controlled by Abs, a former Nazi) and other German and European banks. The EU and its Parliament have no control over the bank or its policy. Monetary policy all around the world is controlled by the world's leading financial institutions. Governments, remember, have no control.

Everyone, it seems, wants to get rid of cash.

First, companies which accept payment by card have to pay commission to the credit card companies. The commission can sometimes be very high with 5% and 7% commission rates not at all uncommon.

Second, clearing banks don't like cash because handling it is time consuming and, therefore, expensive. Moving money around simply by pressing numbers on a keyboard is much quicker and cheaper (though, curiously, the length of time required to move money from one account to another seems to have lengthened since such methods became available).

Third, governments and government agencies love to see citizens forced to rely on digital money because it is much easier to keep control of what everyone is earning and spending when all money goes through computers. So, for example, in the UK the tax office (HMRC) easily obtained details of what taxi drivers are doing by looking at the records from companies such as Uber. When drivers apply to renew their licences, HMRC sends out threatening letters suggesting that they may have made an under declaration or no declaration at all.

And, of course, there are all those individuals who think that using plastic to pay for everything is clever and modern. They don't realise that plastic cards and chips under their skin are enslaving them and removing the last vestiges of freedom.

Any business which relies on a financial trail (e.g. one that uses an e-commerce site) can now be easily monitored by all government departments. And, of course, it is much easier for banks or the Government to cut off an individual's access to their own money if everything is done digitally. And when all money is digital, banks and other financial institutions will be able to charge what they like. Tax authorities will take what they like from your account.

In the new world of digital money, anyone who shares what is labelled 'hate speech' or 'misinformation' will be banned from having an account. (It is, of course, already happening.) All those old tweets, and the time you gave a 'thumbs down' to the WEF, will be marked against you.

Remember how American citizens who gave money to the Canadian Truckers had their bank accounts frozen? If you've ever criticised your government then they will make you pay heavily for your impertinence.

Those individuals who have already lost their PayPal accounts will probably never be allowed to have digital accounts. And without digital accounts they will starve.

It's already becoming nigh on impossible to buy petrol without a credit card. And the number of car parks where cash is still accepted is shrinking fast.

Banks throughout the world are preparing to close down all free thinkers. If you think I'm exaggerating just check out what has already happened.

It has been made clear (by the Bank of England and other clearing banks) that when cash has been replaced with digital currencies, the banks will control how people spend their money. It will be possible to make broad judgements (for example, no one will be able to buy alcohol) and specific ones (patients with early heart trouble will not be allowed to buy certain foods). It will also be possible for governments, banks and companies to monitor spending habits. So, if there is a shortage of eggs for example, the authorities will be able to make sure that no one buys more eggs than they are allowed.

Removing cash from society will make life incredibly difficult (for which read 'impossible') for those who are not computer literate, for beggars and for charities who rely on cash. The quality of our lives will be massively diminished by the disappearance of cash. And, of course, getting rid of cash can be used to track where we go and what we do.

Many local councils are now forcing motorists to use an App available only on a smart phone to pay for parking, and in those places it is impossible to pay for a parking place with cash. The information which motorists are forced to give can be used in many ways (and will be sold for a variety of purchasers so, for example, thieves will know when householders are away from their homes). Forcing motorists to use a smart phone in order to park a vehicle is clearly discriminatory (since it means that those without a smart phone cannot park) and almost certainly illegal.

And, of course, people tend to over-spend when they use credit or debit cards for everything they buy. Using cash helps keep people out of debt.

It's vital to remember that they want to get rid of cash for their benefit and not for our benefit. Removing cash will empower the conspirators and remove, for ever, the last vestiges of our independence.

We really are close to the end as far as cash is concerned. According to data provider Merchant Machine, cash is now used in only 1% of payments in the most digitalised economies in the world, now including Sweden, Denmark, Singapore and the UK. Every time anyone uses a credit or debit card, or flashes a contactless payment card for a small purchase, they are taking us closer to a digital society and digital enslavement.

The end of cash is now just months away.

And when cash disappears it will take with it the last vestige of our freedom.

The restrictions on what we can, and cannot, do with our own money get longer by the day. For example, states within the EU will have to collect information on the ownership of luxury goods such as aeroplanes, boats and cars and each member state will have to establish a 'financial intelligence unit'. Rules in England now make it extraordinarily difficult for citizens to access their own money or even to move it from one account to another.

I recently tried to take some of my money out of my account and was shut in a room and interrogated like a criminal before eventually, and rather begrudgingly, being given an envelope containing the cash I'd asked for.

Even moving from one account to another has become fiendishly bewildering and time consuming.

I was standing in a bank the other day trying to move money from one account to another. I was moving my money from one of my own accounts to another of my own accounts. I don't know if you've tried doing this recently but it gets harder by the week. You need to produce a driving licence or passport, of course. (Heaven help you if you don't have one or the other, or preferably both.) And you need your bank card. And, depending upon the mental state of the cashier, you may need a utility bill, a tax form and a council tax demand. You may soon need a note from your mother.

And, of course, they now have a veritable litany of questions to fire at you. 'Has anyone asked you to make this transaction?' 'Are you under pressure to do this?' And so on and so on. They pretend the questions are to protect us but only the naïve and dim-witted believe that. These stupid questions are devised by very wicked people to delay the whole procedure and to force us all to bank online.

One of the daftest questions is this one: 'Is anyone waiting outside for you?'

Standing next to me, at the neighbouring window, stood a little old lady well, in her nineties. She too was trying to move money from one account to another so that she could pay a bill.

'Is anyone waiting outside for you?' asked the bank clerk.

'Oh yes,' said the little old lady naively. 'My friend brought me.'

The clerk looked as pleased as if she'd won the lottery. 'Oh, well I can't help you then,' she said with a big smile and a sense of satisfaction you could have bottled.

The little old lady didn't understand. 'But my neighbour had to bring me,' she explained. 'I'm 93. I had to give up my driving licence.'

The poor woman didn't understand that logic and honesty are no longer relevant.

'But your neighbour might have put you under pressure to make this transaction,' said the clerk, brim full of sanctimonious, self-righteous, box-ticking obedience.

'My neighbour?' said the old lady. 'Why would she do anything nasty to me? I've known her for nearly 50 years.' She looked around, bewildered. 'I've been banking here for years. Doesn't anyone recognise me?'

'That doesn't matter,' said the clerk, her joy now slightly diluted by exasperation. 'I can't help you if you have someone waiting for you. Those are the rules.' And then she added the killer. 'It's for your protection.'

And so the old lady, puzzled and confused, tottered out of the bank and back to her neighbour's car.

I swear that happened. And I'm not surprised.

(The banks make a great fuss about our responsibilities and their lack of them. But did you know that Barclays Bank has just been fined $361 million by the US Securities and Exchange Commission? And do you know why? Well, they 'accidentally' sold $17.7 billion worth of structured financial products for which they did not have authorisation. The total effect on shareholders (including many pensioners), as a result of this $17.7 billion 'accident', was to help push down net income by 19%. The little old lady's one mistake was that she didn't tell the clerk to move $17.7 billion that she didn't have from one account to another. They'd have done that with a smile and probably given her a free pen and a cup of coffee too.)

Morons (of whom there are many these days) claim, as they have been told, that the inquisition is for our benefit. That's yet another lie. The banks want to force us online. And, as a side effect, they want to absolve themselves from blame when they screw up (which they do on a regular basis). If you want evidence that the banks have been politicised just look at the way that individuals who dare to stand up and question the system lose their bank accounts. In Canada, citizens who stood up in defence of truckers protesting about vaccine mandates, lost their bank accounts. And the same thing is happening with frightening regularity everywhere else. In England, the boss of an independent platform carrying free speech videos lost his bank account and found that no other bank would accept him as a customer. No one could tell him what his crime was. Nigel Farage, the well-known politician, was suddenly told that a bank he had been with for 40 years was going to close his accounts – both business and personal. A man who asked why his local building society was festooned with flags celebrating homosexuality found the cost of free speech when the building society responded to his query by closing his account.

Bank staff seem to have been indoctrinated by the same people who indoctrinated NHS staff, train drivers, civil servants, teachers, council employees and just about everyone else in this increasingly miserable and oppressive world of ours.

(Teachers call what they do 'brainwashing in a good cause'. But can brainwashing ever be defended? If the evidence for their claims were solid and honest they would not need to make stuff up or to attempt to brainwash their students. For decades now, school teachers have been indoctrinating rather than teaching their pupils, promoting the myth of climate change, changing history to meet woke demands and altering the balance of history to suit their propaganda. And refusing to allow pupils to question or debate the official version of history.)

Taking cash out of your own account has become an exercise in patience and determination.

I recently went into a branch of my bank wanting to take out some money – a little more than the machine would allow me to withdraw. I had bills to pay and I wanted to buy some presents.

'Are you going to take this money home and keep it there?' asked the clerk.

I thought this was an incredibly stupid question. The woman was a stranger and she had my address on a screen in front of her. She wanted to know if I was going to take money home and keep it there to be stolen. What an idiot. So I was a little cautious. As any sensible person would, I said 'No'.

'So, why do you want this money?' asked the impertinent bank clerk.

'To buy sweets,' I replied. It has been my standard reply to this question for years.

Bang. I could tell from her eyes that the metaphorical shutters had come down.

You can't make light-hearted comments any more.

The clerk looked at her screen as if it were telling her something.

'Your request has been blocked,' said the clerk.

In full sight of other customers I was ushered into a room and the door was closed.

And I was interrogated. I felt like a criminal. Most people would, I think, have found it a humiliating and embarrassing encounter.

Phone calls were made. I was instructed to answer questions put to me on the telephone. (I couldn't understand the questioner's accent and so I needed a translator.) To check my identity I was asked for my date of birth (a piece of information that is about as secret as Prince Harry's level of affection for his brother).

And eventually, after what seemed like several hours of interrogation, I was, with ill-grace and no apology, given the amount of money I had requested.

It wasn't a loan I was asking for. It was my money.

(As an aside, a week later we had to call a drains expert in to deal with a drain which had been blocked by tree roots. The man dealing with our drains told me, in precise detail, about my experience at the bank. He even knew the precise amount of money I'd tried to take out of the bank. Banks may pretend to care about their customers but there are, it seems, no longer any rules about confidentiality.)

It is, of course, all part of the scheme to force us to bank online – ready for the digital currency they have ready for us.

Your bank hates you. They want to turn you into nothing more than numbers on a computer.

And the staff of banks everywhere are, I fear, too stupid to realise that as soon as the digital currency is here, managed entirely online, then they will all be surplus to requirements. Every last one of them will be joining the dole queue – where they will stay forever, surviving on their Universal Basic Income and living in a small cardboard walled flat the size of a dog kennel.

The idea of providing citizens with a Universal Basic Income, now so popular with governments and conspirators and neoliberals everywhere, is not a new one. During his first year as President of the United States, Richard Nixon announced his 'New Federalism' programme which would provide a Guaranteed Annual Income to all Americans. The proposal would have massively increased the power of the Government. Left-wingers welcomed the idea as an example of 'creeping socialism'. Nixon also suggested a decentralisation programme which was ostensibly designed to spread power to local politicians by handing out subsidies and payments. Nixon announced that he had become a Keynesian. What he forgot to mention was that John Maynard Keynes, the economist, was a socialist whose intention was to promote the 'euthanasia of capitalism'. Like almost all economists who followed him, Keynes was a neo-liberal; an intellectually, emotionally and morally stunted breed without whom the conspirators would have never been able to promote their Great Reset. The chief beneficiaries of the efforts made by the neo-liberals have, of course, been those 'working' in the finance, insurance and real estate sectors of society for those are now where wealth accumulation is taking place – well away from traditionally useful commercial and productive activities. The chief losers have been those involved in making and selling products which people need in order to live and the clear winners have been those in financial services who pay themselves huge bonuses even when their banks are losing money. The global economy is not built on the handling of money rather than the making of things or providing those services which make people's lives better.

21

Much of what is happening is described as progress but it isn't really, of course – it's just change. And a good deal of it is change contrived to keep us all too busy to notice what is going on in the world, and too wrapped up in our own daily problems to take action against the conspirators, the collaborators and the constant attacks on our freedom and humanity. Even small things become incredibly time consuming and exhausting. The bizarre and indefensible 'recycling' programmes which were introduced globally (everything happens in lockstep these days) were designed to make us worry about non-existent climate change, to make us compliant and to force us to accept that we must do what we are told, even in our own homes, and to keep us busy. Most of the carefully washed and sorted recycling material is dumped or burnt, and the environmental cost of collecting recycling material far exceeds any value that might accrue. In the UK, for example, much of the recycling material has been carried to countries far away to be dumped or burnt. There isn't even any point in recycling paper (the most traditional recycling material). It is better for the environment to grow trees for that purpose and to burn the discarded paper to produce electricity or heat.

If you order a book (or whatever else) online you will be bombarded with emails. There will be a message to say that the purchase has been made, one to say that your order is being dealt with, another to let you know that the book has been passed to the delivery company, one to let you know that the delivery company has received the package, one to inform you that the delivery company is preparing to deliver the book, one to let you know that the book is on its way and one to tell you that the package has been delivered. Then you will receive an email from the seller to let you know that the delivery company has done their job and delivered the book. Later there will be another email from them wanting you to rate their service and one from the delivery company wanting you to let them know how well you think they did. If you don't reply immediately those emails will be repeated at regular intervals. This barrage of unnecessary emails keeps us occupied with pointless trivia. (Not infrequently, I receive two copies of each of the emails in this tedious chain.)

The word 'progress' is used as a synonym for 'better'; but how do you define 'better'? Is receiving an email from a friend on holiday better than receiving a postcard? Is the world better when cars all look exactly the same? Is it better when log fires are forbidden by health and safety officials? Are trains better now that there are no restaurant and sleeper cars? Or has life been destroyed by fanatics, cultists and ignorant meddlers, acting, unknowingly, on behalf of conspirators aiming for a Great Reset? Is life better now that there are no junk shops, no rag and bone men and no odd job men who could repair just about anything you couldn't deal with yourself? Is life better now that family doctors work the same hours as librarians and you have to plan your emergencies a day or two ahead if you hope to ride to hospital in an ambulance? Are hospitals better now that nurses spend more time in meetings than on the ward and are always too busy, and self-important, to find a bedpan, plump up pillows, help a frail patient with their meal or put a bunch of flowers into a vase? Is it progress that children now learn with the aid of iPads instead of being taught with pens and paper and chalk and a board? Is a smart phone real progress over a piece of slate and a slate pencil? Children half a century ago played hopscotch, skipped with ropes and in the winter played football with coats as goalposts while in the summer they played cricket with stumps chalked on lampposts. On their summer holidays they splashed in paddling pools or sailed toy yachts on boating ponds (all now filled in for health and safety reasons) and they rode on donkeys and played one penny games on the pier. Is it simply nostalgia when you know in your heart that things really were better then?

If you object to all progress then the conspirators will label you a 'Luddite', even if much of what they label progress isn't progress at all.

It isn't difficult to argue that children have little or no future today. The conspirators and the collaborators have taken away their education, their hope, their sense of comfort and even their happiness. Mental health problems among the young are rising at a rate never seen before. Even before the fake pandemic of 2020 the incidence of such problems among the young was frighteningly high. Today, there is an epidemic of mental illness. Millions of children, teenagers and young people are taking tranquillisers and anti-depressants (even though these have been proven to be of no value) and often taking them for years at a time. The lockdowns, the social distancing regulations and the partial or complete closure of hospital departments mean that those requiring specialist help will be on waiting lists for years if not for life.

Is a pub with a log fire and friendly bar staff better than a pub with a good internet connection? Are motorways, with endless queues, better than winding country roads which take you to your destination just as quickly and with far more pleasure? Are self-driving cars better than cars which have to be driven? How will self-driving cars manage to navigate English country roads and all those tiny, blind junctions? Who is going to provide a suitable call out service for all the electric cars which are stranded in country lanes when their batteries run out?

Is a traditional English breakfast better or worse than a bowl of sugar coated cereal? Why does it now take a week or more for a postcard to reach its destination when in Victorian times, in the 19th century, a postcard put in a pillar box in the morning would arrive at its destination in the afternoon? The postcode or zip code was, surely, an early sign of the end of civilisation. I recently bought around 1,000 old Edwardian postcards (no one wants them these days – they cost just a few pounds) and although the addresses consisted of nothing more than (at most) a name, a number, a street and a town, the cards clearly reached their destinations safely. There is less mail today because so many people use email – so why does the mail take so much longer to get where it's going?

Is reading a book on a smart phone easier and more fun than reading a paperback – with no need to squint and constantly adjust the position of the screen on a sunny day? Was the NHS better when there was a dental service for all? Were charities more or less inclusive when they served merely to serve those in need rather than to enrich executives and advertising agencies? Was life better when we used public phone boxes instead of having to carry a mobile phone with us? Were radio and television programmes worse when traditional events such as the Promenade Concerts celebrated cultural traditions rather than global ones?

Was the Tate Britain art gallery better when it paid more attention to traditional artists than to the demands of the woke? The Tate Britain gallery now has just one room for art from 1545 to 1640 but 14 rooms devoted to art from 1940 onwards. Of the work on view, 200 items were made since the millennium and the work in the publicly funded gallery has been carefully curated to ensure that men and women are equally represented among living artists – regardless of reputation or the value of their work. Modern art on display, representing just a twentieth of the time span of the collection, takes up a quarter of the space. Culture, as well as history, has been changed to fit the requirements of the conspirators and the collaborators. Labels attached to older pictures highlight social injustice, colonial exploitation and prejudice. The gallery seems to illustrate the way in which the feelings of the few now dominate the views of the many in every sphere of activity.

The aims of the WEF and other organisations seem to be to destroy each nation's heritage, to destroy every country's culture. In the UK, all major institutions seem to have become very woke. The National Trust, the Marylebone Cricket Club and other former institutions are now unrecognisably woke – to the great confusion of long-standing members. Long established regiments in the army have disappeared or been merged.

The aim of the conspirators is to change the world by erasing nations, families and communities and by destroying everything humans consider to be personal and valuable. Immigration (whether legal or illegal) is encouraged in order to create impoverishment, resentment, racism, terrorism and plenty of excuses for war. (As an aside, it used to be thought that patriotism was good but nationalism was bad. Today, however, both are unacceptable because there can be no countries in the New World Order.)

Naturally, immigration programmes have led to resentment on both sides and, especially in France, the development of racial and cultural ghettoes is leading to civil war.

22

In this book I will show how the United Nations, the Round Table, Black Lives Matter, the Democrats, the Republicans have destroyed our lives with the controversies over gender (with insane gender language changes being introduced with the sole idea of creating confusion and destroying human relationships), transgender politics (also designed to bewilder and create division) and exaggerated campaigns against sexual abuse ('He said my hair looked nice', 'He said he liked my dress' 'My life is now ruined'). A wolf whistle used to be regarded by most women as a compliment, today it is a criminal offence. The conspirators have deliberately created division, distrust and fear between the sexes, and the neoliberals who run the global economic system have consistently shown that their aim is not to create more fairness, or to advance the rights of women in those countries where unfairness is commonplace, but to create as many divisions as possible between men and women. The aim of the neoliberals who make up the Establishment, and who are pushing us towards their beloved Great Reset, is to break up society in as many ways as possible so as to ensure that men and women are too busy fighting one another to worry about the progress towards the New World Order. It is for this very same reason that national history and national and regional culture are being banished from every aspect of life, and why schools and colleges no longer teach students material which could be construed as patriotic or in any way likely to lead to greater pride.

23

Then there are the absurdly exaggerated accusations of racism, always popular with communists who see such accusations as a way to break down society, with accusations built on the flimsiest of pretexts ('He couldn't pronounce my name properly and so he is a racist', 'He didn't pick me for his team and so he must be a racist'.) A well- known personality had to issue a grovelling apology after people with too much time on their hands found that he had once sent a tweet commenting that he perhaps needed to learn another language when he was in London. Since most people in London aren't native to England and don't speak English at all or very well, his remark was well based and logical. But it was wrongly perceived as being racist because the person who saw it as racist had been encouraged to want it to be racist.

The attempts to outlaw racism themselves produce racism, of course, with affirmative action and positive discrimination being nothing more than racism of another colour. Appointing a black woman to a company board of directors simply because she is black and female, and helps the company hits its diversity quota, is racist and sexist and just plain wrong. The black woman should be appointed because she is the best candidate and will do the best job for employees, shareholders and customers.

Advertisers who show photos of happy couples or families invariably show a black couple or a black man and a white woman (usually a blonde). It is now uncommon to see any white men appearing in print or television advertisements. This isn't simple political correctness but is done because it enables the advertiser to avoid any accusations that it might be racist. It is virtue signalling and it is actually racist of course.

I read recently of the existence of an 'initiative' in the UK called 'Black Farmer's New Face of Farming' with a range of food products called 'The Black Farmer'. In the United States there is an organisation called Black Farmers' Market. And there are a number of trade organisations along these lines. There is, for example, a National Black Police Association and in London there is the Metropolitan Black Police Association. There is a Black Writers Guild, a Black Writers Society and a Black Writers' Association. And there is a Black Agents and Editors' Group. I can't help thinking that by defining a group according to skin colour these no doubt well intended individuals are sustaining and even creating racism. And I wonder what the reaction would be if a group of farmers founded an organisation for white farmers. Or if a group of white policemen founded an association called the White Police Association. I find it difficult to avoid the suspicion that creating racial groups in this way is part of the conspirators' plan to create disharmony in society.

In June 2023, it was revealed that the RAF has been practising discrimination against white men. 'Discrimination' is, of course, just a polite word for 'racism'. If a black man is unfairly treated because of his skin colour it is racism and there is an uproar, sackings and scandal. If a white man is unfairly treated because of his skin colour it is discrimination and no one cares. There seems little doubt that if racism is a serious problem in the UK it is white men and women who are most commonly the victims.

We see footballers and other sportsmen kneeling in an attempt to show their moral integrity but merely displaying just how easily they can be manipulated. They seem to me to be displaying shallow fake compassion and their own propensity for virtue signalling. When it comes to the crunch, however, the sportsmen seem sadly short of moral courage. At the World Football Cup in Qatar, for example, male footballers bravely announced that they would wear a rainbow armband during the tournament to show their support for homosexuals. (For unknown reasons, homosexuals have stolen the rainbow, long a Christian symbol, as an emblem. And homosexuality is outlawed in Qatar. One might have thought that a better and more fitting way of expressing their feelings would have been to refuse to go to Qatar at all.) However, when the organisers announced that footballers wearing rainbow armbands would be sanctioned, the footballers all abandoned their enthusiasm and put away their rainbow armbands

24

The Bank of England (which is responsible for making a mess of the English economy and failing to control inflation) has said that people of any 'gender identity' (I think they mean men or women but who knows) can be treated as pregnant. And the Bank is having some gender-neutral lavatories built so that lady bankers and gentlemen bankers who aren't sure of their gender identity can go to the loo together and share the experience in politically correct harmony. The Bank's insane pregnancy policies mean that anyone can now be classified as a birthing parent and claim family leave from the bank. I bet there are some people facing 7% mortgages who wish the Bank would concentrate on inflation and worry a little more about the economy and a little less about showing how wokey it is.

There are endless attacks on masculinity and femininity with constant pressure towards unisex washrooms and a unisex world. We can only stand and watch the banishing of the family unit and the rise of the State as a central factor in our lives, the prejudice and dishonesty of the mainstream media (which now seems to specialise in misinformation and disinformation and rarely, if ever, reports the news without a built-in judgemental commentary), the rise of homosexuality and the remainder of the specialities within the LGBTQIA community. (I tried to find out what the Q, the I and the A stand for but failed in this simple task. No one I spoke to knew the answer, and even the internet was unable to provide an answer.).

It used to be considered polite for a man to offer a co-worker or friend a compliment ('Your hair looks nice', 'That dress suits you' and so on) without anyone being offended. Indeed, if the compliment were a genuine one the recipient would be pleased and flattered. Today, such remarks are considered to be signs of extreme sexist behaviour and men have been fired for saying such things and branded as sex offenders. It is even now considered sexist for a man to stand up on public transport and to offer his seat to a woman, or to allow a woman to proceed before him through a doorway. (Ironically, men may sometimes be accused of being rude for not doing these things.)

And, of course, those promoting women's professional sport are insisting that as much attention be given to female football and cricket teams as to the more traditional male teams. Huge amounts of money are being funnelled into female sport even though the evidence clearly shows that there is very little spectator interest in matches played between women's teams or indeed when individual women play sports (women have been playing professional tennis and golf for decades but the interest in their games has always been minute when compared with the interest in male versions of those games.) The media, as always, has been supine and some newspapers now give more coverage to women's sports than to men's sports with the result that their readers find it nigh on impossible to navigate their pages. A casual reader will see a headline that screams 'England World Cup Triumph' and will find themselves reading about the success of a team of 14-year-old girls playing lacrosse or netball.

Once again, there is a hidden agenda.

Promoting and encouraging sexism encourages conflict and confusion – two essential building blocks regarded as essential for pushing us into the Great Reset. And new rules about 'equality, diversity and inclusion' have replaced humanity, goodwill and kindness with statutory obligations, statutory whingeing and statutory recriminations. The rules about diversity, inclusion and equality are doing far more harm than good. You can't regulate for kindness.

Something called the Independent Commission for Equity in Cricket (commissioned by the England and Wales Cricket Board in a mood of self-flagellation) caused a storm (and a good many headlines) by complaining that racism, sexism, classism and elitism are widespread in the game of cricket.

I've been following cricket all my life. I have spent a huge chunk of my life on cricket grounds. I've spoken to many cricketers. And I've been inside professional dressing rooms as a doctor. I've written four books on cricket (including *The Village Cricket Tour* and *Thomas Winsden's Cricketing Almanack*) and I've written a column and articles for specialist cricket magazines. And I believe the ICEC report will do far more harm than good.

But I wasn't in the slightest surprised by its conclusions. The death of cricket has been on the cards for some time. After all, some of those involved with the dangerously fascist Great Reset, the climate change myth and the absurd re-wilding nonsense want to stop all sport because it takes up too much space and involves travel.

To me the ECB's report stinks of woke gibberish.

Equity in cricket, for heaven's sake. That's a real ESG word.

The woman who was chairman of the committee is described has having experience in 'governance, inclusion and equity'.

What a surprise.

A woman described as a senior independent director of the ECB said: 'Promoting equity, diversity and inclusion across the game is critical to the success of our game-wide strategy Inspiring Generations and our purpose of connecting communities through cricket.'

Rishi Sunak, a well-known war criminal, took time off from sending depleted uranium shells to Ukraine to get in touch with the ECB. He wants cricket to be inclusive and open to everybody. I actually rather thought it was. Even blind people play cricket.

I think they've all missed the point. (If I'm allowed to have a view on this – which I rather fear may not be the case these days.)

Cricket isn't a social programme or an experiment in human resources.

Cricket is a game. Or I thought it was.

If people want to play they play. If they want to watch they watch. If people from some areas of society aren't interested then that's fine. There are plenty of other games they can play. Cricket doesn't exist to change society and lead us into the Great Reset.

The report makes it look as if cricket had huge problems.

I don't believe it does.

At least, I don't think it did.

I think this report could create some very big problems and it is my belief it could do more harm than good.

They won't agree with me, of course, but I fear this report will exacerbate suspicions, paranoia, resentment and entitlement and actually create racism.

If you look at tennis, rugby, football, gymnastics, chess, dominoes or synchronised swimming through the same distorting spectacles, you could claim they all have problems. There are far more black players in top level professional football than makes statistical sense. How many black tennis players are there in local tennis clubs? How many Muslim women are there involved in synchronised swimming? Enough? Not enough? Too many? Who decides?

The report says that there must be a 'fundamental overhaul of the women's pay structure in order to achieve parity with the men's game'.

I'm terribly sorry, (and this really isn't a sexist comment, it's a realistic comment) but that is like saying that the members of the chorus in an opera should be paid the same as the lead tenor and soprano.

Look at the stands when women are playing. There are huge empty spaces.

If women are to be paid the same as men then the men will have to take a huge pay cut. There certainly isn't enough money in the sport to pay men and women the same as the men currently receive.

The report says that Black cricket has not been adequately supported.

Black cricket?

I thought teams had black and white players together. Gordon Greenidge and Barry Richards were probably the greatest opening partnership in history. One was black and one was white.

Are we now going to have black teams and white teams?

The report says that 'cricket needs to have a clear set of values'.

No it doesn't need a set of artificially created values.

Cricket needs some laws. Which it has. And it needs players to play the game fairly and honourably. Which they mostly do. That's where the phrase 'it's not cricket' came from.

What on earth do they mean anyway?

The 317-page report says that costs are prohibitive.

Really?

Have they looked at the costs of getting started in motor racing or horse jumping? Or skiing? Or yachting?

Do they want taxpayers to provide every child with a free bat and ball?

Kids who want to play cricket need an old tennis ball, a piece of wood and a lamp-post on which to chalk the wickets. And someone to play with.

And look at this quote from Ben Stokes, the England cricket captain, made after the absurd and damaging report was made public: 'I am Ben Stokes, born in New Zealand, a state-educated pupil who dropped out of school at 16 with one GCSE in PE. I needed help with the spelling and grammar in this speech and I am sitting here as the England men's Test captain.'

Elitism?

Where is the elitism?

The truth about cricket is that most of the people who play it and watch it are rather decent. They don't play or watch to change society. They play or watch because it's fun. They enjoy it. And the last thing most people think about is skin colour.

It isn't the fault of cricket that the money grubbers sold the TV rights to a satellite TV company – thereby ensuring that kids don't watch it and aren't interested in playing.

It isn't the fault of cricket that local authority schools don't play much cricket. That's because local councils sold off the playing fields to developers.

There's sexism, racism and old-fashioned snobbery in all corners of life.

But cricket isn't any worse than anywhere else though I admit there isn't a Test series for transgender cricketers and there obviously should be.

This accusatory and adversarial report commissioned by the ECB seems to me to be full of modern 'Great Reset' language: intersectionality and cisgender make an appearance, of course.

The report apparently criticises the fact that some who watch cricket don't like drums being played all day long. Well if I watch cricket I rather like it to be a peaceful activity. Is that now a race crime? Drums and impromptu bands and noisy behaviour should be banned. May I say that, please?

And the report criticises the huge number of cricket followers who dislike the Hundred – which is a daft form of biff bat cricket rather too similar to French cricket for my tastes. I want the Hundred (which is, I believe, destroying county cricket) to be forgotten about. Am I allowed to say that?

Are we now to be told what sort of cricket we can enjoy?

Oh, and the report talks about 'Type K' individuals.

'Type K' people are, apparently 'white men, educated in private schools, who are straight and cisgender and do not have a disability'.

I would like to think that this utterly awful report will go straight into the bin. And the ECB which commissioned the report should also go in the bin.

But they won't.

I fear that 'action' will be taken and the death of cricket will get ever closer.

Cricket has been painfully woke for some years now. The annual *Wisden* seems to have become woke. And I think the MCC is pretty woke too.

And, thanks to this report, I suspect that things are now going to get much worse.

The overall plan, espoused by the climate change enthusiasts, is to stop all sport – both amateur and professional – because it takes up land which they believe should be used for rewilding and because it involves travel.

25

The project known as Environmental, Social and Governance (ESG) is a dangerous and enormously damaging form of woke capitalism, which is used as a weapon by governments, banks and regulators and even promoted with religious fervour by brokers, analysts and financial journalists. ESG is, without a doubt, doing far more harm than good and is part of the conspirators' plan to ensure that 'we own nothing'.

Larry Fink, the chairman and chief executive of BlackRock (which is an investment company) says, rather bizarrely, that 'access to capital is not a right. It is a privilege' and has warned that corporate 'behaviours are going to have to change, and this is one thing we are asking companies; you have to force behaviours and at BlackRock we are forcing behaviours'.

Fink is not a politician or an elected official but the company he runs has control of trillions of dollars' worth of investments. His role as a money manager means that he has a fiduciary responsibility to those whose money he looks after.

Fink's outrageous arrogance and hubristic determination to claim power beyond reason has, fortunately, aroused some opposition from those who don't accept that Mr Fink has the right to bully the directors and staff of other companies or to take decisions on behalf of shareholders. In Florida, US, the Governor, Ron DeSantis, has signed into law a bill which prohibits state officials in Florida from investing public money to achieve ESG goals.

Meanwhile, outside Florida, those who doubt or question ESG are cancelled and likely to lose their credit rating. Corporate doubters will be excluded from bond markets and forced onto the fringe of corporate society. The three biggest credit rating agencies have added ESG ratings to their portfolios, and so every company in the world has to obey the demands of the ESG enthusiasts. Companies which produce hydrocarbons (such as oil companies) have great difficulty in borrowing money and shareholders have lost their rights as company owners.

Fink believes that climate change is real (despite the evidence that it is not), that children in kindergarten schools should be taught about sex, including homosexuality (despite the opposition of many parents), and that everyone (boy or girl) should be free to use whichever loo they prefer (despite the opposition of almost everyone of both sexes).

Fink appears to believe that companies should ignore their shareholders and adopt something called stakeholder capitalism – something which means giving power to lobby groups and elites and creating a new form of socialism whereby other people's money is distributed to the poor and used to pursue the policies Fink feels are most important. In order to ensure that his policies are followed, Fink pushes through changes in company policy, and by bullying and pushing hard to promote his pet theories, ensures that boards of directors include members with extremist views. (Anyone with investments might like to consider Fink's attitude when deciding whether or not to allow BlackRock to manage their investments.)

Fink isn't quite alone in his determination to take over the world, of course. Michael Bloomberg, another extremely arrogant fellow, and a man who runs a financial media company which provides news for most of corporate America, seems to have similar aims, and both men could not unreasonably be described as being egotistical, narcissistic and megalomaniacal. Two men with but one Napoleon complex. Another man with similar enthusiasms, Doctoroff, is Bloomberg's media boss. And some, at least, of these views seem to be shared by Hank Paulson, a former boss of Goldman Sachs and Tom Steyer, a hedge fund billionaire.

Bloomberg is also much convinced by the fake climate change industry and has provided free prosecutors to sue energy companies if he doesn't like them.

By pushing their propaganda very widely, these people have massive influence on climate science researchers and they influence the multi-billion dollar a year climate industry.

Sadly for Fink and Bloomberg, a growing number of experts are prepared to speak out and tell the truth about subjects such as climate change. 'Dodgy science published by climate advocacy groups is certainly not uncommon,' said Roger Pielke, a Professor at

University of Colorado. And Warren Buffett, the legendary investor has also expressed scepticism. The evidence shows that their illogical obsession with Net Zero will lead to billions of deaths from disease, starvation and other preventable problems.

26

Starvation is being created quite deliberately as part of the plan to reduce the world's population.

Encouraged by cultist-controlled politicians, vast quantities of the world's crops of corn, soy bean and so on, are being used to make biofuels so that motorists can continue to buy cheap petrol for their motor cars. A while ago, a list of 51 things you and I can do to prevent global warming was published. Number 1 on their list was headed 'Turn food into fuel'. This, it was claimed, would have a 'high impact' on the global warming problem. It was suggested that ethanol is the alternative fuel that 'could finally wean the US from its expensive oil habit and in turn prevent the millions of tons of carbon emissions that go with it.'

This is dangerous nonsense. When more land is used to grow biofuels, so that 'green' motorists can drive around feeling virtuous, there is less land for growing food and an increase in the number of people starving to death.

The demand for biofuels has been soaring for years (despite the knowledge that, as a result, people are starving) and the increased use of biofuel is a major force behind the rise of food prices. If greens keep promoting biofuels then there is going to be a global shortage of food and millions are going to die as a result.

There are other problems with our food supplies, of course.

Big American seed companies have been busy patenting the rights to many individual seeds. They have done this so that they can force farmers around the world to buy their products. One result has been that small farmers in India are no longer allowed to grow seeds from crops that their families have been planting for generations. If they do, then lawyers for American multinationals will smother them with writs and injunctions.

As a result, the incidence of suicide among small farmers in developing countries is terrifyingly high.

Finally, large modern farms are remarkably (and surprisingly) inefficient. When the fuel used to build tractors, make fertilisers and pesticides and so on is taken into account, it turns out that the energy cost of a kilogram of corn has actually risen in the last few decades. Soil erosion, the loss of pollinators (such as bees) who have been killed by chemicals, evolving chemical resistance by pests and numerous other environmental problems have also reduced farm crops.

The result of all this is that food is becoming scarce and prices are rising. This is not a cyclical change (with prices falling or rising due to changes in the weather). It is a structural change and it is, I fear, permanent.

As far as food prices are concerned, the conditions really are optimum for a 'perfect storm'. At first glance it appears that things really couldn't get much worse.

But, actually, they could.

American genetic engineers have been 'modifying' food for years to make it more profitable. No one knows what effect their modifications will have on the safety of food for human consumption. No one knows what other horrendous side effects there might be. The risks are unbelievably dangerous. So, for example, if every farmer in the world grows the same 'brand' of potato and that potato is hit by a deadly disease then there won't be any potatoes.

For those in Europe and America all this is not yet critical.

But for those in many other parts of the world this is already an outright disaster. In some countries nearly half of all children are malnourished. And things are getting worse and will continue to get worse. Rising prices and falling quantities of food available for eating (as opposed to filling petrol tanks) will result in massive starvation around the world. The fake coronavirus hoax, and the consequent economic problems which will devastate economies everywhere, will exacerbate the problem. As a result, the incidence of global starvation is set to rocket.

It's no good saying that the planet isn't overcrowded (it isn't) or that there is plenty of food (there is), for the inescapable fact is that as a result of policies controlled by international organisations controlled by the United States of America, at least five million infants and small children die each year – in a good year. That figure is set to rocket in India, Nigeria and the Congo and elsewhere. The number of people in extreme poverty around the world could soon double to over 200 million.

Increasing agricultural production enabled the world to grow from 1.7 billion people to nearly 7 billion people in just a century. But when the oil runs out, the world will not be able to feed that many people. The oil is needed for farming as well as for transport.

The racist and elitist policies of the climate change enthusiasts who want us to stop using oil will, if they are successful, be responsible for billions of deaths.

The billionaires assume that they know best about everything (because they are rich) and that the end always justifies the means. Their arrogance has also helped them become ever richer. In the last two decades billions of dollars have moved from the middle classes to the billionaire classes. Real wages have been falling and the value of savings, investments and pensions has fallen steadily while the billionaires such as Fink and Bloomberg have got ever richer. It is difficult to avoid the feeling that Fink and Bloomberg have for years now been on a very effective mission to destroy American from within.

The unavoidable truth is that everything needs energy and without energy everything stops. The climate change believers have pushed energy costs ever higher and if they are able to understand even the simplest scientific evidence, they must know that renewables will never replace carbon based fuels. However, it is largely thanks to the efforts of Fink, Bloomberg and their billionaire colleagues that capital spending on fossil fuels has fallen dramatically and fuel production has dropped 30% since 2020.

27

The wilful destruction of pensions through absurd political shenanigans, the monstrous nonsenses known as diversity and sustainability, the rise in the power of the central banks and the Bank for International Settlements are all closely linked, all carefully designed, and all have exactly the same long-term aim: a World Government and a global population of serfs (with the World Government almost certain to have its parliament building in Israel which may be one of the most unstable and aggressive countries on earth but which is also the physical or spiritual home of many of those leading the demand for a Great Reset and a World Government controlled by and for bankers and billionaires). Incidentally, civil servants and those with publicly funded pensions might think that their retirement is well-funded because they have been promised good pensions. I'm afraid that they are deluding themselves. No publicly funded pension is safe.

28

The illiterati, the truth deniers, the conspirators and the collaborators have invented a language of their own. By looking for their favourite words you can easily identify the conspiratorial globalists.

And so here are their favourite words. If you see more than two of these words in any document then you know you are dealing with a conspirator. You should be aware and wary.

Collaboration: The conspirators love to pretend that they are part of a big, happy family of individuals who have seen they are light. In fact, of course, they are collaborators in the way that thugs who set fire to a tramp in the street are collaborators.

Sustainable: This is probably their favourite word. They can't usually manage a paragraph without using it at least once. Everything has to be sustainable.

Resilient: They use this word a good deal when talking about risk management.

Leadership: The collaborators like to think that they all have leadership qualities. They don't have any leadership qualities, of course, and so they use the word a good deal when describing themselves and their colleagues. The words 'common purpose' are also popular among those who consider they are following the 'play book'. (The illiterati are also very keen on 'toolkits' and 'group think' though none of them has the foggiest what these mean.)

Impact: They use this word to show the effect of one of their social engineering programmes.

Denier: They use this word to describe anyone who does not share their insanity. It is used as a term of abuse. If they call you a denier you should be proud.

Inclusive: The collaborators love to feel that they are inclusive. They are fans of forced homogenisation. They believe in mixed loos and mixed sports teams because these are a true sign of inclusivity.

They like to subordinate individual rights to the rights of the community.

Equity: The conspirators are huge fans of the redistribution of resources – as long as they get more of whatever there is than anyone else. It is through their enthusiasm for 'equity' that the collaborators show their allegiance to the communist cause. They also like to move towards the standardisation of everything.

Diversity: They love this word even more than they love the concept. Everything must be diverse. They believe in the deliberate and steadfast disruption of what they call 'organic patterns of association'. If you want to imitate one of the globalists just talk about diversity and sustainability.

Transparency: The globalists are firm believers in transparency when it comes to other people. They are, for example, enthusiastic supporters of 'track and trace'. But they are not as keen about transparency when it comes to themselves and their own dirty deeds.

The conspirators and collaborators are also desperately enthusiastic about accountability as far as it relates to other people. They always like to create permanent digital records of everything other people do. They insist that everyone (except themselves) should be accountable for their actions. They themselves steadfastly refuse to debate the value of what they do.

Innovative: They love this word because it makes them seem original and creative. Sadly, of course, none of them has ever had a single original or creative thought. They prefer to follow the playbook devised by Schwab and the other leaders of the Nutter Movement. They talk a good deal about the Fourth Industrial Revolution because this makes them sound like intellectuals. (Naturally, most of them have no idea what it means and didn't even know there were three other industrial revolutions until last week.)

There are other words to look out for, of course. Words such as 'predictive', 'profiling' and `standardisation' invariably crop up at least once in every document they produce. And remember too, of course, that the illiterati who believe in global warming and the Great Reset regard a document of 500 pages as a short note.

29

The battle between individualism (the essence of humanity and freedom) and collectivism is vast and continuing. The collectivists are enthusiastic promoters of mass vaccination programmes which are offered not to protect individuals but to protect communities, with no scientific evidence that they do either and much evidence that they do lasting harm. We are being moved towards a four day week (at most), job sharing, working from home (guaranteed to reduce productivity) and, as jobs become scarce and people decide they don't want them anyway, a State paid for, State sponsored, State selected universal basic income. Everything that is being done to oppress and suppress us is promoted and protected by, it seems, all the world's lobbyists, pressure groups and self-appointed fact checkers.

30

The quickest and easiest way to become rich these days is to set up a fact checking company. You can easily persuade huge companies to hire you to 'fact check' anyone telling the truth. I have investigated a number of fact checkers specialising in scientific matters and found that none of them had any relevant qualifications and all of the ones I found merely labelled anything which contradicted the conspirators' official line as 'fake news'.

Describing yourself as a 'fact checker' is one of the quickest way to riches these days because there are many large organisations which are ever eager to hire fact checkers and are, seemingly, unconcerned about the qualifications (or lack of) of the individuals concerned. I decided that the word 'deception' is the collective term for fact checkers as in: 'a deception of fact checkers'.

One of the fact checkers I encountered (by accident rather than design) was someone called Dave who edited a website called Media Bias Fact Check. Dave described his site as 'the most comprehensive media bias resource on the internet'. He claimed to have five volunteers to help him and admitted that none of his team was a professional journalist. Dave said he 'currently works full time in the health care industry' though he didn't say whether he was a brain surgeon or a hospital car park attendant or a drug company sales representative. He described himself as an armchair researcher and boasted that his website had been used as a resource by BBC News, among many other media organisations.

I found that like most fact checkers, Dave was quick to describe videos and articles as 'FALSE' (fact checkers always put that word in capital letters, as though it has more gravitas that way) or as containing 'misinformation', even though everything in a video or article had been thoroughly and professionally researched.

When I examined his fact-checking site, Dave appeared to have based his judgement on material which appeared on a site called Politifact which itself contains errors. They said I had a Facebook video. But I have never had a Facebook account. They said that in 2019 I authored a book aimed at discrediting trust in vaccines. That's not true either. (The only book on vaccines which I have written was published in 2011 and it was aimed at providing readers with facts.) They report that there is no clear evidence that the coronavirus vaccines have killed or will kill anyone. I don't think I'm the only doctor in the world to disagree with that. Indeed, how can anyone write that a drug will never kill anyone?

Another fact checker claims they wrote to me c/o the email address on my website. There is no email address on my website.

Dave didn't like another video of mine called 'Doctors and Nurses giving the covid-19 vaccine will be tried as war criminals.' He labelled that one FALSE, based on yet another fact checker called Lead Stories.

The problem with that judgement is that the eighth word of the title of the video is 'will', suggesting that something is going to happen in the future. It is, of course, impossible to label such a judgement as false unless you have direct access to the future.

31

Progress in terms of people getting richer relies on productivity going up but the opposite has happened in recent years. Inflation, soaring taxes, lockdown mentality, working from home and other factors are pushing people into giving up in despair. Millions now choose to live on benefits, retire and take their pension early, or choose to be classified as long term sick and give up work for the rest of their lives. In the UK there are, as I write in the summer of 2023, four or five million people classified as long term sick – people who are officially allowed to remain off work for the rest of their lives. (Precise figures are always difficult to obtain from governments but when figures are offered they are invariably massively underestimated.)

32

By the summer of 2023 there was some belated discussion in the press about whether lockdowns had helped prevent the spread of covid. In fact there is no doubt that the lockdowns made the situation considerably worse and were responsible, as I predicted when they were first introduced, for hundreds of thousands of deaths.

What is ignored, however, is that the lockdowns were not introduced to stop the spread of covid-19. The lockdowns were introduced as a form of compliance training. Their subsidiary aim was to make people so lonely and despairing that would be ready to grab at any solution. And the solution, of course, was the toxic and experimental covid-19 vaccination.

33

The innocent and the naïve believe that everything is happening by accident. Farmers around the world seem constantly bewildered and confused by policies and decisions which are designed to please the enthusiasts, calling for the closure of farms in order to appease the psychopaths calling for net zero. In an article in a British magazine (which, like others, seems to have fallen for the Green myths with all the mindless commitment of a teenager in love) one leading Green academic recently said 'Farming has no option – it will have to be sustainable, otherwise it will not be sustained' and there were doubtless many Green heads nodding though I confess I was merely left puzzled.

Confused farmers describe new government policies as vindictive, senseless, cruel, destructive, insane, bureaucratic, dangerous and just plain bewildering. Farmers are encouraged to follow 'biodynamic' farming methods whereby herbal and mineral preparations are used together with an astronomical calendar to guide sowing and harvesting dates. (I'm not kidding.) Nowhere is there more incomprehensive jargon than there now is intruding into the world of farming. Many farmers have been pressured into supporting the absurd re-wilding programme which is promoted with such enthusiasm by the climate change believers. The conspirators' plan is to reduce the amount of land available for growing food in order to create food shortages, starvation and a consequent, inevitable reduction in the size of the global population. The aim is to allow between a third and a half of all land to go wild. Even parks are being allowed to grow wild, and gardeners are encouraged to let their grass grow throughout the summer. Re-wilding is leading to grass being left long and uncut on verges, in public places and private gardens.

So what's the underlying reason? (They always have a reason.) Well, long and uncut grass will dramatically increase the spread of ticks and the incidence of Lyme Disease. It will also increase the number of people bitten by adders. If you don't see an adder and you tread on it then it will probably bite you. And all that long grass will dramatically increase the amount of hay-fever. Plus, long, uncut grass on road verges and traffic islands makes road accidents far more likely. Re-wilding is part of the plan to make everyone miserable, ruin everyone's health, make money for the drug companies and kill a few people.

In order to ensure that neither farmers nor members of the public encroach on land which has been set aside for rewilding (and the first re-wilding programme was introduced by the European Union some years ago in a scheme which was called 'set aside') wild animals are being released. In England, for example, bison, water buffalo, wild boar and beavers have been introduced with predictably disastrous results. The naïve assume that if land is left uncared for, fields will become wild flower meadows, full of daisies, tulips, forget-me-nots, snapdragons, violets and other wonderful delights. In reality, of course, fields which are abandoned to the re-wilding scheme simply become a chaotic and unpleasant mixture of nettles, brambles, dock and giant hogweed with outbreaks of Japanese knotweed growing rapidly over the years to come.

Today, most farmers see their problems occurring as a result of stupidity, ignorance or a failure to understand their needs. But what is happening to them is nothing to do with stupidity, ignorance or a failure to understand – it's all deliberate and quite cold blooded. More and more European countries are now dependent on imports for most of their food and energy supplies.

The bottom line, vital to remember, is that nothing is happening by accident or by coincidence.

The same things are happening in all industries and all professions but because people tend to see only their own small area of activity most don't realise that their confusion, their own horror story, is part of a wider pattern that affects all industries, most professions and all nations. The patient who spends two years on a waiting list for surgery is suffering (and probably unable to work) not by accident but by design. The traveller whose journey is disrupted by delays and strikes is suffering because of planned delays and well-organised strikes. The parents whose child is not being properly educated should understand that the educational system isn't failing by accident but by design. We all need to see everything that is happening as a part of a plan, rather than as a series of isolated incidents. My purpose in writing this book is to put everything in context and to enable the reader to see things in perspective, and later in the book I will explain how we got here and who is responsible. There is a greater plan, the plan for the Great Reset, and it is being executed with military precision.

34

And then, inevitably, came the designer war, ostensibly between Russia and Ukraine but in reality between America and its NATO satellites and Russia.

It is clear that President Putin didn't want to sell his country to the American juggernaut, driven by the conspirators, and that was enough to mark him as an enemy. It also seems clear that NATO and Russia were involved in a battle to decide which of them would control the world government which both of them are expecting. NATO and Russia were playing a massive game of Monopoly, with the prize being control of much of the world's resources rather than the rent on a few wooden houses and the penalty being almost complete annihilation rather than a request to pay £200 to the bank and an instruction not to go past 'GO'.

Everything bad that happens has been deliberately organised by American politicians and bankers. What we are seeing now is a culmination of a process which started well over 100 years ago and is now rapidly approaching fulfilment. We now live in a world where bankers, who produce nothing, who are of no real value to society and who unquestionably do far more harm than good, control the world's money.

35

Today's problems aren't caused by the fact that 1% of the population controls most of the world's property and wealth but by the fact that the 99% are, through their mortgages and bank loans, in debt to the 1% and many will spend their lives working to pay off those mortgages or loans and, at the end of their lives, end up no richer than they were to start with. The 1% (or, in fact, considerably less than 1% but I'll stick to calling them the 1% because it's a simple way to describe them) have taken control of the 99% because, to put it bluntly, they own them. The 1% has sucked the world dry of money. They control everything. They control natural resources, they control finance, they control the politicians, they control the judiciary, they control the police, they control health care and they control the military. Globally, they have virtually total control over organisations such as the United Nations (and its subsidiaries such as the World Health Organisation), the World Bank and the International Monetary Fund. Any dissent that appears at the top is contrived and artificial. The 1%, the conspirators, may sometimes appear to be at war with a government or an administrative body or an NGO but they are never at war with anything or anyone because they control everything and everyone. The 1% controls the protestors. Black Lives Matter, climate change groups and mobs smashing store windows are all financed by the billionaire financiers.

36

Nothing is at it appears to be and nothing, for sure, is as the media would have us believe. Everything you read, see or hear courtesy of the mainstream media is a lie. For example, the mainstream media around the world insisted that Russia had destroyed its own Nord Stream pipeline even though there was excellent evidence that the pipeline had been destroyed by the Americans – whose president had, indeed, boasted that the pipeline would be destroyed. There was of course no logical reason for the Russians to destroy an enormously expensive pipeline, and if they'd wanted to stop the flow

70

of gas to Germany they could have merely turned off the supply. When the Kakhovskaya hydroelectric dam was destroyed, the BBC's first reaction was to blame the Russians, even though there was, once again, no logical reason why the Russians should destroy a dam which was providing water for much of Crimea and was essential for the functioning and safety of their own nuclear power station. Moreover the area beneath the damaged dam was largely occupied by Russians. All the evidence showed that it was Ukraine which benefited from the dam's destruction. Even after Russia had accused Ukraine of destroying the dam, the mainstream media continued to blame Russia, with most mainstream outlets refusing even to mention the far more likely possibility.

Modern, Western societies were originally designed to stop anyone taking control. The legislative branch of government was kept separate from the other branches simply so that all the power would not be in the hands of the few. But the 1% has changed all that. Moreover, the 1% has achieved this position simply by manipulating the money and by using the money to control the politicians. I wonder how many people know, for example, that after the banking collapse of 2008, which started in the US and became global, it was American President Obama who decided not to prosecute any of the bankers who had created the crash. It was President Obama, a Democrat ostensibly representing the ordinary men and women of America, who defended the bankers, who insisted that the millions of people who lost their homes should not be bailed out and who arranged for bankers such as Goldman Sachs and J.P.Morgan to be bailed out with billions of dollars of taxpayers' money. Furthermore, it was President Obama who allowed the bankers to use the bail-outs to give themselves huge bonuses. And yet the mass of people still revere Obama, the great betrayer, and regard him as a hero. (The banks were presumably grateful and it is, of course, merely a coincidence that former President Obama became strangely wealthy after his term as President came to an end.)

37

Democracy (once described as the tyranny of the majority and abhorred by Socrates, Plato and Aristotle) has, like much else, been weaponised and a new breed of woke individuals (who believe they are exhibiting compassion which, in truth, they neither feel nor understand) show a sense of reverence for the spiritual trimmings of the State that marks them out as being indistinguishable from the brain-washed followers of Mao Tse Tung. They are just as blind to truth, decency and respect as the committed followers of any dictator in any totalitarian regime must be.

All these things, and many more, were and are connected by a long-running conspiracy of bankers, politicians and assorted billionaires; a long running, deep seated conspiracy which this book exposes and defines in great depth and detail.

Today, there is an understandable inclination to regard the fake coronavirus pandemic that was used to bring in lockdowns, social distancing, mask wearing and pseudo-vaccines, as the start of the troubles which are destroying our world and taking away all vestiges of our freedom and humanity.

But all that has been nothing more than an exercise in compliance training, designed to terrify, to subdue and to force billions to forget everything they know, to ignore all truths, however blatant, to set aside all natural suspicions, and to become obedient serfs. What has been happening in the last three years (the fake plague, the nonsense of net zero and all the accompanying restrictions, the beginning of World War III) is merely the culmination of something that started many decades ago.

Everything is hotting up because the conspirators, the very few men and women who are behind everything that is happening, can smell the fear and taste the blood; they know that the mass of people are broken and can easily be controlled. They know too that this is their moment; if they pause or hesitate then they are lost and it will be decades, at least, before they have another chance.

When we are afraid we do not think properly and when the fear becomes chronic our ability to think clearly is suspended more or less permanently. We have been manipulated and groomed for decades; trained to be fearful. The threat of the nuclear bomb, a range of threatened infectious diseases (starting with the wildly exaggerated threat of AIDS), constant wars around the globe, the madness of the wildly exaggerated threats that the world will end in five years, ten years, fifteen years or whatever because of the non-existent threat of non-existent climate change, endless over-promoted distractions, accusations of racism, sexism and so on – all these have created fear, depression and increasing despair. Just as Carl Jung had predicted, the State has taken the place of God.

The conspirators know that people in fear need and demand someone to take control. Adults become like children, requiring authority and tolerating surveillance that would otherwise be regarded as intrusive. People become ready to sneak and snitch on their fellows. The most absurd instructions are followed without question. And so, because of the threat of an imaginatively marketed flu, the elderly were locked in care homes for years, and relatives were only allowed to see them through glass. Vaccination programmes were promoted with bizarre incentives (in America it was possible to win $5 million if you agreed to be vaccinated, and free beer and free doughnuts were given to those who had been jabbed). Celebrities offered abuse to those who questioned the need for the vaccination programme. The Queen of England and the rest of her family exhorted everyone to be jabbed. The Archbishop of Canterbury promised that those who were jabbed would be loved by Jesus (and, presumably, those who didn't get vaccinated wouldn't be loved). The BBC told the public that the covid-19 vaccine was safe and effective – though the medical evidence at the time showed clearly that the vaccine was neither of these things and the assurances were offered without any scientific background.

The truth is that the vaccine damages immune systems, making those who have had it more likely to catch (and die from) other infections. And will the covid-19 jab affect the fertility of those who had it? It seems very likely. Cancer rates are rising rapidly among those who agreed to be vaccinated. It was clear in the autumn of 2020 that the covid-19 jab would be neither safe nor effective, and today there is now no doubt the covid jab is a killer, fake vaccine – useless but far more dangerous than depleted uranium shells or cluster bombs. Like bombs, rockets and bullets, its only conceivable purpose is to kill people.

The evidence showing that the over-promoted, over-sold covid-19 jab is the most dangerous pharmaceutical product ever used is denied only by fools or shills for the conspirators and the drug industry. I have repeatedly warned that the covid jab can and does cause or exacerbate a huge range of serious health problems – including heart disease, clotting problems and cancer. And as I warned in 2020, the immune system problems caused by the 'vaccine' are deadly.

The evidence suggesting that the covid vaccine is toxic is overwhelming and should be banned is constantly growing. Any other product known to cause such severe problems would have been taken off the market a long time ago.

A review of 325 autopsies on patients who died after covid vaccination showed that 74% of the deaths were caused by the covid vaccine.

The nine eminent authors of the paper found that the organ systems most likely to be involved in covid jab deaths were: cardiovascular system, haematological system and respiratory system. The mean time between vaccination to death was 14.3 days. A total of 240 deaths out of the 325 deaths were independently adjudicated as directly due to or significantly contributed to by covid-19 vaccinations.

The nine authors concluded: 'The consistency seen among cases in this review with known covid-19 vaccine adverse effects, their mechanisms and related excess deaths, coupled with autopsy confirmation and physician-led death adjudication, suggests there is a high likelihood of a causal link between covid-19 vaccines and death in most cases. Further urgent investigation is required for the purpose of clarifying our findings.'

Then there was the paper which appeared in the *British Journal of General Practice* recently which showed that 'enlargement of axillary, supraclavicular or cervical lymph nodes following vaccination with covid-19 mRNA vaccines is more frequent than initially reported, with a rate reaching up to 16% following the second dose of the Moderna mRNA vaccine.' The paper also reported that a few cases of lymphoma were reported in the literature.

The authors warned that doctors in charge of patients with post-vaccination lymphadenopathy should be reminded to consider the possibility of an underlying or coincidental malignant disorder. The truth, of course, is that there aren't enough doctors around to check fully 16% of all the patients who have a second dose of that vaccine.

The covid jab is causing one problem after another. And the problems are ignored or suppressed by the medical establishment.

In July 2023, I showed that the covid-19 jab was responsible for a surge in type 1 diabetes among children and teenagers.

A survey of 38,000 young people (reported in the *Journal of the American Medical Association*) showed that the rise is substantial.

I warned that this would happen back in 2020. I warned that the covid-19 jab would push up blood sugar levels.

The epidemic of type 1 diabetes is caused by the covid-19 vaccine. And the drug companies will now get ever richer selling treatments for diseases the drug companies caused.

Everywhere you look there is evidence proving that the covid jab was a killer. In less than two and a half years nearly 2,000 healthy athletes have had heart attacks or sudden serious health problems – with over 1,300 of them dying.

And yet, in the summer of 2023, the medical establishment, bought with drug company money, was still refusing even to contemplate the idea that the deaths may be caused by their beloved vaccine. They didn't dare admit that the medical profession was responsible for thousands of unnecessary deaths because they were terrified of the inevitable lawsuits not to mention the professional embarrassment.

It was clear that doctors who gave the covid jab without properly assessing the dangers were going to be on the wrong end of the world's most expensive class action lawsuit.

But the vaccines have not been withdrawn. No one in the drug companies or the medical establishment issued grovelling apologies.

Instead, as had happened for over three years, the doctors who were exposing the dangers of the covid-19 jab were being harassed, banned and censored.

Any doctor who was still giving the covid-jab had shown themselves to be a dangerous fool who should be struck off the medical register for life and arrested immediately for attempted murder.

38

It is, of course, possible to trace the plan to control the world back hundreds of years.

In *The Republic*, Plato recommended creating a super-state headed by philosopher-kings. Charlemagne wanted the world, and not just Europe, and who knows where Napoleon's ambitions would have ended. Thomas More wanted Utopia and Alfred Lord Tennyson wanted much the same. H.G.Wells took time off from writing excellent novels to toy with the idea of a global super-state.

Those planning the conspiracy have always had a long-term plan but they also knew that they would, in their lifetimes, benefit enormously from their conspiracy.

The conspirators may think of legacies and dynasties but although they like nothing more than to be described as philanthropists, they are not individuals who think much of the concept known as altruism. The conspirators are men and women who believe very firmly that charity begins at home. The conspirators do not do things just because they are the 'right things' to do. If they make a donation to a college or a hospital or a foundation of some kind they insist that the recipients put their name on a building, a scholarship or some other memorial. If they have a foundation then they will find a way to benefit from the foundation's tax-free status. These are people who, by and large, know that they cannot be immortalised in statue form, because everyone who saw the statue would say: 'Who the devil was he?', and so they force themselves onto the future in a more modern, practical way.

39

All the events I have described so far are linked in which can best, and most appropriately, be described as global terrorism on a scale never previously seen – let alone imagined.

Now it's time for some explanations and some revelations.

It's time to go back over two centuries to the end of the 18th century when the House of Rothschild was operating in Europe and when they created the basis of their wealth by financing wars.

The Rothschilds didn't finance one side in a war. They didn't give financial help to governments, kings or leaders of whom they approved; they financed both sides. In wars they financed all the armies involved and made profits from everyone. During the 19th century, wars led (as wars always do) to a rebalancing of power. And at the heart of the power sharing sat the Rothschilds.

The founder of the dynasty, Meyer Amschel Rothschild, who operated out of Frankfurt in Germany, was a crafty and rather greedy man who had five sons, four of whom he sent to various parts of Europe to organise financing in England, France, Austria and Italy. The fifth son stayed in Germany.

It has been said that the Rothschilds weren't merely profiteering but were behind all the wars in Europe in that time. Millions of people died so that the Rothschilds could become rich. And with their wealth came power.

How did this bunch of crooks make their money?

Simple.

Wars cost money, lots of money, and the Rothschilds were always there with bags of gold to pay for soldiers and guns and ammunition. Whenever there was a battle there was always one certain winner: the Rothschilds. They lied, and deceived and tricked their way to becoming international bankers. And, of course, to becoming incredibly wealthy. They got rich by lending money to all the politicians and all the kings and charging them huge amounts of interest.

In the American Civil War, the Rothschilds helped finance both sides. I wonder how many American children hear about that in their history lessons.

Wars cost huge amounts of money and in the end, of course, it is a country's taxpayers who have to find the cash. Financiers like lending money to governments because they know that they can charge a high rate of interest, they know that they will almost certainly get their money back and they know that if a government owes them money they will probably be able to do advantageous deals giving them monopolies, and the freedom to exploit natural resources such as areas containing oil or metals.

This way of working was gradually copied by other bankers, and by the 21st century it was becoming clear to anyone who looked that when US troops stayed in a country after an invasion, they weren't there to help but to steal natural resources. (Examples included Iraq, Libya and Syria.) The American style was to create a war between two sides, send in troops to help whichever side they thought most sympathetic to the American cause (or whichever side had the best natural resources or wealth) and then steal whatever natural resources (oil, gold, other minerals, antiquities or money) which the country had.

77

Today, no one likes to say much about the Rothschilds for one simple reason: they were Jewish. And organisations such as the Anti-Defamation League have always regarded any attack on Jewish bankers as being anti-Semitic. Academics, authors and journalists are always careful about mentioning the role Jewish bankers have played in the development of what is without doubt a global conspiracy because of the danger of being classified, and attacked, as anti-Semitic. This is, of course, absolute nonsense. Drawing attention to the actions of the Rothschilds and other Jewish bankers has nothing whatsoever to do with the Jewish people as a whole. But for the conspirators it is convenient, quick and effective to use the anti-Semitic insult as a defence weapon to silence historians and honest commentators.

In fact, Jews should be as angry as anyone about the actions of the Jewish bankers. In World War II for example, the Warburgs, a Jewish banking family, helped to finance Adolf Hitler and the National Socialist Party. If you want to know more about the role of the Warburgs take a look at Zina Cohen's *The Shocking History of the EU*.

Newly minted international bankers (such as the Rothschilds) didn't just make vast amounts of money out of wars and governments, they also acquired extraordinary amounts of power. So, for example, governments gave the bankers the right to form central banks. The Bank of France, the Bank of Germany, the Bank of England and, in America, the Federal Reserve were set up not by governments but by bankers with their own interests at heart.

The story of how the Federal Reserve was created is extraordinary. A bunch of leading American bankers took a trip to Jekyll Island in Georgia and created America's central bank in secret. The story of this chicanery is told in G Edward Griffin's 600-page book *The Creature from Jekyll Island: A Second Look at the Federal Reserve*. The bankers were aided in obtaining control of America's money by a man called Colonel Edward Mandel House who was English and no more a colonel than Colonel Tom Parker, Elvis Presley's manager. Colonel House was a behind-the-scenes fixer who wrote about establishing 'socialism as dreamed by Karl Marx' in America and who wanted a central bank which could provide flexible, inflatable paper currency and a graduated income tax. House was said by some to be more powerful than President

Woodrow Wilson and this does not seem at all far-fetched. With House running the economy, America's national debt expanded by 800 per cent.

In an attempt to disguise their perfidy some of the bankers behind the plan for the Federal Reserve pretended to oppose it. New laws were passed which appeared to control the bankers but which actually gave them more money and more power.

A similar system has been operated by the European Union for decades. The eurocrats who create the EU's laws appear to be defending ordinary people by devising yet more laws and regulations to control banks and businesses. In reality, the laws and regulations are introduced at the behest of lobbyists working on behalf of big banks and big international companies and they are part of the plan to create a global financial system, a global currency and a global government. The powerful men and women who pay the lobbyists (not all of them bankers or financiers) know that the rules and regulations will make it impossible for new companies (and banks) to get started in business. Large companies, on the other hand, will ensure that the EU creates laws which don't actually affect their earnings. And, of course, they will hire huge departments full of specialists who can use the new legislation to their advantage. All this is aided by the fact that there is an easy movement of staff between the EU and the large companies the EU is supposed to regulate. There has never been as corrupt an organisation as the European Union. Back in 1995, Brian Freemantle wrote an astonishing and revealing book called *The Octopus* about corruption in Europe. My own more recent book *OFPIS* contains revelations which I still find astonishing. It is not surprising that the media and the British civil servants are strong supporters of the EU since they are all strong advocates of a world government and all that goes with it.

The real socialists, and the real communists, who welcomed the way the bankers appeared to be working (and the central banks they created) had no idea that they were being manipulated and controlled by very rich, very crafty, men whose plan, even then, was a world government which they would control.

And those who were surprised that rich bankers should support the idea of a progressive income tax did not realise that the bankers (and their rich friends) would not be paying the tax for they would use foundations, trusts and offshore tax shelters to protect their wealth. And so individual bankers actually owned their countries' central banks and had the power to create money and control those countries and their populations. It was Lenin who said that establishing a central bank was 90% of turning a country into a communist country and, indeed, having a central bank is one of the ten requirements listed in The Communist Manifesto. It isn't surprising that Thomas Jefferson wrote that 'banking establishments are more dangerous than standing armies'.

Even after the Bank of England and the Bank of France were theoretically brought under political control (and 'socialised') the bankers who had originally been the owners retained power over them. Montagu Norman, the longest serving Governor of the Bank of England (he held the post from 1920 to 1944) was described by the *Wall Street Journal* as 'the currency dictator of Europe'. Norman, who was by any standards a 'bad' man, boasted 'I hold the hegemony of the world'. In 1942, Norman was quoted as saying that 'the hegemony of world finance should reign supreme over everyone, everywhere, as one whole super-national control mechanism'.

Today, the central banks have enormous power. In the US, the Federal Reserve controls interest rates and the money supply and can, therefore, decide whether there is going to be a recession or a boom. It is the Federal Reserve that decides what happens to share prices and it is the Federal Reserve which decides whether Americans have to deal with inflation or deflation. The plan behind the formation of the Federal Reserve was always a simple one: to enable billionaires to pretend to introduce a socialist state, a workers' democracy, so that they could control the country and become dictators.

The bankers had also realised that if they created artificial panics they would have even more power and make even more money. By scaring ordinary investors (and pushing them into selling their shares, for example) they could make enormous profits. And bankers have manipulated and controlled entire countries since the early years of the 20th century. It was J.P.Morgan, the eponymous founder of one of the world's most powerful banks, who created panic in order to ensure that the Federal Reserve was created. It was Morgan who pushed the US into the Great War in order to protect loans he had made to the British Government. Woodrow Wilson had been re-elected as President after promising to keep America out of what was seen as an exclusively European war. But while Wilson was busy promising that America would not get involved in the war between England and Germany, Colonel House was forging an agreement with England to do just the opposite. The men who had been at the Jekyll Island meeting, and who had created the Federal Reserve, were keen to become involved because many of them had lent money to England and were keen to ensure that their money was not lost. And, of course, there was plenty of opportunity for businessmen to make money out of the war. Bernard Baruch alone fixed up government contracts worth tens of billions of dollars. The mainstream media was told to switch from opposing entry into the war to saying that it was essential for America to become involved. Authors Gary Allen and Larry Abraham reported that one British MP, Arthur Ponsonby, wrote that 'there must have been more deliberate lying in the world from 1914 to 1918 than in any other period in the world's history'.

Tragically, it now seems clear that the decision to push America into the war did far more harm than good and it was certainly the beginning of America's long period of being involved in wars between other countries. (America has been at war with someone, somewhere pretty much since 1914. The bankers, the financiers and the arms manufacturers need constant war.)

Bankers and arms dealers made fortunes. However, Winston Churchill noted that everyone, everywhere would have been better off if the Americans had stayed out of the war. He argued that peace would have been made with Germany, that there would have been no collapse in Russia leading to communism and no collapse in Italy leading to the rise of Mussolini and fascism. Most importantly, perhaps, the Nazis would have never been able to take power in Germany if the Americans had stayed at home and a settlement had been agreed between England and Germany. The negotiators at Versailles, who allegedly sorted out the peace settlement after WWI knew damned well that it was going to make things worse rather than better. And remember what happened to the Middle East and the attempt by T.E.Lawrence (Lawrence of Arabia) to provide the Arabs with a fair solution.

Lord Curzon remarked that the Versailles treaty was 'not a peace treaty'. He described it as 'simply a break in hostilities' and he was, of course, absolutely correct in his assessment.

Not long after the end of the Great War ('the war to end all wars' and not, then, of course, given a number) the American bankers were lending money to a German politician called Adolf Hitler. And during the Second World War, American companies were providing the Nazis with essential supplies. Moreover, even before the end of World War II, the insiders were carving up Europe and planning more wars.

(Incidentally, many Americans, particularly those who lost loved ones in the Vietnam War, might be surprised to learn that the Viet Cong and the North Vietnamese received 85% of their arms from Russia and Soviet Bloc countries and that those suppliers were helped by American bankers and industrialists. Once again the conspirators in America were financing and equipping both sides of a war and providing the enemy with the bullets which were killing American soldiers. The rules said that American companies couldn't sell 'strategic' weapons (such as guns) to the enemy, but they could sell the tools to make the guns. The Vietnam War was fought without there having been a formal declaration of war and so the financiers could not be arrested for treason.)

The end of the Great War provided the bankers, the fixers such as Colonel House and the other insiders with a real chance to set up a world government. And so the League of Nations was created. The problem was that everyone involved in the negotiations knew that everyone else present was cheating and lying and no one trusted anyone. The Americans huffed and puffed and walked out and the proposed World Government fell apart.

Not everyone in America had given up, however.

The ubiquitous Colonel House met with members of The Round Table and the Royal Institute of International Affairs and the Council of Foreign Affairs. Their plan was to try to work out a way to persuade the voters of Europe and America that they needed a world government to guarantee peace.

Meanwhile, after J.P.Morgan's death it was his bank which helped to finance the Revolution in Russia.

Most people assume that the Russian Revolution developed because lots of poor, hungry people in Russia got very angry about the fact that the Czar and his family were enjoying great riches and 15 course meals while they were scrabbling around looking for bits of stale bread to dip into some brackish water. It is assumed that angry mobs smashed their way into the palace and attacked the Czar.

The problem with this story is that Czar Nicholas II abdicated seven months before the Russian Revolution took place. And Nicholas II stood down under pressure not from a mob of Russian peasants but from the United States and England. To make the whole thing look like a rip roaring revolution, the infamous so-called leaders of the revolution were taken to Russia. Lenin was sent into Russia on a train with millions of dollars in gold. (That was organised with the help of Max Warburg, the Jewish banker who was close to the Germans and who helped pull many German soldiers from the Eastern front to kill vast numbers of British and American soldiers.)

In order to make the revolution look convincing, Leon Trotsky left America with an entourage of nearly 300 revolutionaries and a good deal of donated money. Trotsky was united with Lenin and the two of them 'created' the revolution in Petrograd. Jacob Schiff, who helped finance Trotsky, is estimated to have spent $20 million on helping the communists take control on behalf of the American bankers. Another financier of the Russian Revolution was a man called Lord Alfred Milner who, with Lord Rothschild, headed a secret organisation called The Round Table. The Round Table's main aim was to establish a world government so that rich financiers could run the world – pretending to do so under socialist control. The Round Table was closely associated with an immensely powerful organisation called the Council on Foreign Relations.

After their success, the Bolsheviks said a big thank you to their banker supporters by transferring vast amounts of Russian gold to Schiff's firm in the United States. And Americans took huge profits from Russian minerals. It was all a very profitable exercise. Some American citizens might be surprised to hear that Stalin said that the United States had helped the communist government considerably. He said that two thirds of all the large industrial enterprises in the Soviet Union had been built with the help or technical assistance of the United States – much of it provided by the Rockefellers and other long-term conspirators. This happened at the same time as the communists were calling for the destruction of the American way of life.

More importantly, America and the West had manufactured an 'enemy', and governments had an excuse to spend billions on manufacturing arms to defend themselves.

It was all horribly easy to organise.

Between 1923 and 1929, the Federal Reserve increased the supply of dollars by nearly two thirds. At the same time the mainstream media promoted shares with tremendous enthusiasm and, as a result, the stock market soared. A major stock market crash was planned in 1927 and the Federal Reserve Board worked with the heads of central banks in Europe to make sure that everything went according to their plan. What happened next is no secret. Thousands of investors were ruined in the crash of 1929. The bankers got richer. Many of them had sold 'short' and made fortunes out of the crash they'd helped create.

And the same scenario is repeated at irregular intervals.

The bankers start a scare.

The frightened investors sell their shares cheaply.

The bankers buy the cheap shares and make a fortune. They are never punished in any way for their dishonesty and greed. (For example, if you want a quick guide to the crash of 2008, I recommend the film *The Big Short*.)

Alternatively, by starting a rumour that a specific company was in financial trouble, the bankers could start a panic, buy the shares sold by panicking investors and then make a fortune. The bankers did that often too. Except for artists of one sort or another, very few people ever get extremely rich honestly. Behind every great fortune there is a history of theft, deceit and chicanery. The insiders who run countries and start wars manage the markets, establish monopolies, control natural resources (such as oil and essential minerals), fix prices, control the labour market and buy and sell politicians.

And, of course, anyone exposing the truth will be dismissed as paranoid, condemned as a conspiracy theorist and labelled discredited.

This has been going on for well over a century. And it is still happening today. Financial markets are regularly manipulated. Central banks (which often appear to be run by incompetent people) force debts higher, play with interest rates in a way that destroys economies and push up inflation when it suits them and the big banks. (When interest rates rose rapidly in the UK in 2023 and people with borrowings were paying 7% or more, savers were still receiving less than 1% in interest. It was clear this was profiteering, shylocking, and that the plan to impoverish everyone was being followed precisely.) Recessions and depressions appear periodically as and when required. The bankers, and the central bankers, know that only precious metals such as gold and silver hold their value.

As Lord Curzon and Winston Churchill had both foreseen, the Great War was not the end of European hostilities. In 1939, the Second World War began. Hitler was helped by the Round Table Group since it was generally felt among the insiders that a Second World War would make it easier to start a world government with the bankers and other insiders running things, and the people of the world being turned into drones. (For more about the financing of the Second World War I suggest that you read Zina Cohen's book *The Shocking History of the EU*.)

As soon as the Second World War started (and years before America became involved) the insiders in the U.S. set up a Committee on Post-War problems. And it was this group of American crooks (aka Wall Street movers and shakers) who set up the United Nations with the plan that this would, at last, lead to the development of their beloved world government. The people involved in the formation of the United Nations included Nelson Rockefeller and a man called John J.McCloy. Nelson Rockefeller is well known but McCloy not so widely known.

McCloy, a former president of the World Bank, had been a partner in a law firm which represented the American portion of German company IG Farben and subsequently acquired a reputation for having sympathy for the Nazis. For example, early in the Second World War, McCloy used his influence to block attempts by Jewish organisations to persuade the US Air Force to bomb Auschwitz because he knew how crucial the concentration camp was to German Industry. It was known that it would have been easy for bombers to destroy the gas chambers and key railway junctions but McCloy (who was, at the time, the Assistant Secretary of War) claimed that bombing Auschwitz might annoy the Germans and provoke them into vindictive actions. Some found it difficult to understand precisely what 'vindictive actions' he had in mind. And it was

McCloy's actions after the end of the War which helped create the European Union.

After the end of World War II, McCloy became US High Commissioner for West Germany. In addition to releasing many industrialists who had been sentenced to prison, he also arranged for Nazi camp doctors and SS officers to be released or to have their sentences substantially reduced.

As soon as McCloy had arranged for their release, the executives from IG Farben quickly re-joined German companies, with, for example, Schmitz joining the board of Deutsche Bank. McCloy was never subjected to serious criticism for any of his actions because he was obeying American instructions. Although President Eisenhower had wanted to rid Germany of the influence of the Nazis, there were other powerful Americans who felt differently. Allen Dulles, John Foster Dulles and General Patton all wanted the Germans to control Europe as a bulwark against the Soviet Union.

After the War, McCloy served as chairman of the Chase Manhattan Bank and the Ford Foundation. (Thomas McKittrick also became a director of Chase Manhattan; a bank which had had strong links with the Nazis during the War.) McCloy also became chairman of the Council on Foreign Relations and an adviser to five American Presidents. In 1963, McCloy, the man who had worked with the manufacturer of the gas which had been used to murder millions of Jews and who had ordered the early release of some of Germany's worst war criminals, was presented with the Presidential Medal of Freedom by President Lyndon B Johnson.

It was entirely thanks to the efforts of people such as McCloy and McKittrick that Schmitz, Krupp and other war criminals (who were as responsible as Hitler, Himmler et al for the horrors of the Second World War, and the efficient brutality of the Nazi war machine) received no punishment at all or the sort of punishment usually regarded as suitable for small time motoring offenders. It was released war criminals who helped found the European Union.

Being much richer than Rudolf Hess, and having more powerful friends, Krupp, who had been sentenced to 12 years imprisonment at Nuremberg, was released by the American McCloy after just three years in prison. It is worth recording that Krupp's imprisonment does not sound much like punishment. A room in the prison was set aside so that the Krupp directors could discuss corporate business, and Krupp was supplied with the best food and wines available. He apparently took delight in insulting the people who had been responsible for his incarceration. Incredibly, McCloy even arranged for Krupp to be pardoned and his record as a war criminal expunged after his release.

Krupp's industrial empire had controlled slave labourers in 57 concentration camps and Krupp, who was also Hitler's Minster of Armament and War Production, was close to the German high command. He was responsible for transferring factories from occupied territories to the German Reich. He was one of the most evil members of the Nazi regime and was awarded medals by Hitler for keeping up production of arms through the use of slave labour.

McCloy later explained his pardon for Krupp by claiming that the German was a 'playboy' who had not had much responsibility. In fact, Krupp had been very much a hands-on operator, and running the companies had been entirely his responsibility. Astonishingly, McCloy even ordered that all of Krupp's property, which had been confiscated after the War, be restored to him so that he suffered not at all. After his release and pardon, Krupp, one of the richest and worst German war criminals, quickly became a seemingly 'respectable' German citizen accepted by German society and playing an important part in the enriching of Germany and the development of the European Union.

It was McCloy who helped the Nazis set up the European Union after the end of World War II.

And, of course, he was one of the Americans who helped to found the United Nations.

The Communist Party instructed its members that 'Great popular support and enthusiasm for the United Nations' policies should be built up, well organised and fully articulate. But it is also necessary to do more than that. The opposition must be rendered so impotent that it will be unable to gather any significant support in the Senate against the United Nations Charter and the treaties which will follow.'

And so the Communist Party supported, endorsed and promoted an organisation (the United Nations) which had been set up by a bunch of American bankers.

Naturally, the mainstream media managed to convince people that the new organisation was set up to promote world peace and most of those now promoting its activities, and parroting the official line, do so without knowing precisely what lies behind the propaganda. Since its formation, the goal of the United Nations has been to abolish all individual countries. And American Presidents have remained loyal to that goal. In 1992, President George Bush said: 'It is the sacred principles enshrined in the United Nations Charter to which the American people will henceforth pledge their allegiance.' Not, you will note, the American flag.

So, now we know where the United Nations came from.

And, more importantly, we know that the United Nations was set up by American bankers and the Communist Party and its aim is to set up a world government. This helps to explain the behaviour of the UN in recent years. All those individuals who thought that the UN was merely a kindly organisation set up to promote the sort of gentle world peace loved so much by Miss World contestants can think again.

Oh, and it is, of course, important to remember that the World Health Organisation, the promoter of face masks and pseudo vaccines which are dangerous and don't work, is a subsidiary of the United Nations.

And now, to find out in more detail how we ended up in a nightmare world, read Part Three and I will explain exactly what has happened and why and who is responsible.

But, before we get there, I have included a short interlude of illumination.

Part Two

Interlude

I have collected the quotations which follow during the last few years. At first, I intended to sprinkle them throughout the text. And then I thought I'd just leave them out. But eventually, I decided to include them in a special section as a prelude to the next part of the book.

'The first thing that we ask of a writer is that he shan't tell lies, that he shall say what he really thinks, what he really feels.' – *George Orwell*

'When you know the enemy's plans, it will be easy to gain victory by means of an appropriate response.' – *Miyamoto Musashi*

'All warfare is based on deception…To subdue the enemy without fighting is the acme of skill.' – *Sun Tzu*

'Power is not a means; it is an end…The object of persecution is persecution. The object of power is power.' – *George Orwell*

'The United Nations represents a potential threat of very great magnitude.' – *Charles Lichtenstein (former US Ambassador to the United Nations)*

'The evidence is compelling that reconsideration of the world monetary system is overdue. Therefore, national economies need monetary coordination mechanisms and that is why an integrated world economy needs a common monetary standard, which is the best neutral inflationary coordinating device. But, no national currency will do – only a world currency will work.' – *President Ronald Reagan, 1983*

'Paper is likely to be abused, has been, is, and forever will be abused, in every country in which it is permitted.' – *Thomas Jefferson, on fiat currencies*

'James Madison said 'It is a universal truth that the loss of liberty at home is to be charged to the provisions against danger, real or pretended, from abroad.' Fear of foreign perils, Madison realised, can easily persuade a freedom-loving people to voluntarily part with liberties they would otherwise consider indispensable.' – *William J. Watkins Jr*

'Sometimes I wonder if the world is run by smart people who are putting us on, or by imbeciles who really mean it.' – *Mark Twain*

'The first panacea for a mismanaged nation is inflation of the currency; the second is war. Both bring a temporary prosperity; both bring a permanent ruin. But both are the refuge of political and economic opportunists.' – *Ernest Hemingway*

'Of course we can split genes. The question is can we not split genes.' – *Jean Paul Sartre*

'Give me four years to teach the children and the seed I have shown will never be uprooted.' – *V.I.Lenin*

'My Government is the world's leading purveyor of violence.' – *Martin Luther King*

'(Politics) is all about sincerity. If you can fake that, you've got it made.' – *George Burns*

'News is what somebody somewhere wants to suppress, all the rest is advertising.' – *Lord Northcliffe*

'There is no such thing as society. There is only the market.' – *Margaret Thatcher*

'Perceptions become reality.' – *Henry Kissinger (after Niccolo Machiavelli)*

'When you have eliminated the improbable, whatever remains, however improbable must be the truth.' – *Sherlock Holmes via Arthur Conan Doyle*

'Naturally, the common people don't want war; neither in Russia, nor in England, nor for that matter in Germany. That is understood. But, after all, it is the leaders of the country who determine the policy and it is always a simple matter to drag the people along, whether it is a democracy or a fascist dictatorship, or a parliament, or a communist dictatorship. Voice or no voice the people can always be brought to the bidding of the leaders. That is easy. All you have to do is tell them they are being attacked and denounce the peacemakers for lack of patriotism and exposing the country to danger; it works the same in any country.' – *Hermann Goerring*

'It was on the advice of Governor Rockefeller, who described Mr Kissinger as 'the smartest guy available', that Mr Nixon chose him for his top advisor on foreign policy.' – *US News and World Report, 1971*

'The history of the twentieth century can best be understood by coming to the realisation that for the first time in the course of human events, the whole world has come under a single idea. This idea, which goes by many names and under many guises, always ends up in some form of collectivism, which crushes the lives and aspirations of individuals in its utopian quest for heaven on earth.' – *Donald McAlvany*

'To parody the words of Winston Churchill, never have so many been manipulated so much by so few.' – *Aldous Huxley*

'It is forbidden to kill; therefore all murderers are punished unless they kill in large numbers and to the sound of trumpets.' – *Voltaire*

'Those who would give up essential liberty, to purchase a little temporary safety, deserve neither liberty nor safety.' – *Benjamin Franklin*

'The people never give up their liberties but under some delusion' –

Edmund Burke

'If you do not fight for right when you can easily win without bloodshed; if you will not fight when your victory will be sure and not too costly; you may come to the moment when you will have to fight with all the odds against you and only a precarious chance of survival. There may be even a worse fight. You may have to fight when there is no hope of victory, because it is better to perish than live as slaves.' – *Winston Churchill*

'With stupidity the Gods themselves struggle in vain.' – *Friedrich Schiller*

'The atmosphere of hatred in which controversy is conducted blinds people. To admit that an opponent might be both honest and intelligent is felt to be intolerable.' – *George Orwell*

'The world is governed by very different personages from what is imagined by those who are not behind the scenes.' – *Benjamin Disraeli*

'Man's dearest possession is life. It is given to him but once, and he must live it so as to feel no torturing regrets for wasted years, never know the burning shame of a mean and petty past; so live that, dying, he might say: all my life, all my strength were given to the finest cause in all the world – the fight for the Liberation of Mankind.' – *Nicolai Ostrovsky*

'Doctor, there is no place for an ill old woman or an ill old man anywhere in this world – if they lack money.' – *Andrew MacAllan*

'Truth lives on in the midst of deception' – *Friedrich Schiller.*

Part Three: How things got the way they are

Introduction

In the introduction to his brilliantly researched book *The Greening: The Environmentalists' Drive for Global Power*, Larry Abraham (who wrote the book with Franklin Sanders) explained that he had for 30 years observed and chronicled numerous onslaughts which were designed to reduce the sovereignty of the individual and transfer more power to our governments. And he warned (and his book was published in 1993 so the warnings were made three decades ago) that the greatest surrender of liberty in all human history was underway and that power was being transferred to a small group of people – the Establishment.

Abraham pointed out that every one of the projects designed to take away our rights and give them to our governments was promoted as 'necessary' or 'vital' and that some were touted as 'life-saving'.

He explained that a well organised minority somehow managed to create 'the appearance of popular support' for projects designed to 'preserve the environment' or 'stop pollution', and that the people behind these programmes were members of a small group.

He quotes Arthur Selwyn Miller, a former Professor of Law at George Washington University who wrote: 'Those who formally rule take their signals and commands not from the electorate as a body, but from a second group of men (plus a few women). This group will be called the Establishment. It exists even though that existence is stoutly denied. It is one of the secrets of the American social order.' And he added. 'A second secret is the fact that the existence of the Establishment – the ruling class – is not supposed to be discussed'. I would add that most of the people involved in promoting the myth of climate change are probably intellectually undersized and possibly clinically insane.

Even thirty years ago the climate change campaigners were 'steamrolling all opposition, silencing critics by a feigned moral and intellectual superiority, and, in the process, transferring global wealth and power on an unprecedented scale'.

Well-intentioned but misguided people, manipulated and tricked into believing carefully constructed lies, now protest about the environment, and instead of marching for peace (as happened in the 1960s) they are campaigning, with increasing venom, against man himself. They fly around the world in their tens of thousands (without ever seeing the irony in what they are doing) to listen to speeches from skilled manipulators who have arrived at the conference venue in their private jets. They have been lied to repeatedly, and brainwashed into believing that man-made climate change is our greatest enemy. Anyone who dares to refer to the true science, and who questions the lies, must be attacked, demonised, cancelled and silenced.

The misguided thousands are told to say that there must be no debate because there is no doubt but in reality there must be no debate because if there were a debate then it would quickly become very clear that the Emperor is naked and everything the public has been told about man-made climate change is a lie. Anyone who questions their myth and their lies, and who dares to argue that man-made climate change is not a real threat, will be demonised and dismissed as discredited.

On the other hand, those who promote the myth are applauded and well-rewarded for their obedience (and stupidity).

Abrahams pointed out that the dedication of well-meaning people was being manipulated (with phony data) and that while endless billions of dollars of public money was being spent, fortunes were being made.

Today, exactly the same lies are being told in the Americas, in Europe, in Asia and in Australasia. Politicians and media commentators everywhere are sticking to the script they have been given and, unquestioningly, repeating every lie they've been told to repeat. Any politician who dares to step out of line is immediately crushed.

'What's happening in the 'environmental' movement is not a zero-sum game,' argued Abrahams thirty years ago. 'There are winners and losers on a vast scale.'

In this section of this book I will show how ruthless bankers and financiers have, for many decades, systematically taken over all the world's institutions, and how they have deliberately and cold-bloodedly used the mythical threat of climate change to begin a process which will, if not stopped, almost certainly lead to a totalitarian world government and the deaths of billions. The conspirators behind the climate change myth want to control all natural resources. They want all the power and all the money. And to achieve their aims they will destroy every aspect of human life that stands in their way: they will destroy family life, culture, history, patriotism and religion. They will destroy pride, respect and caring because they see these as annoying and potentially expensive weaknesses. The leaders of this massive lie, mainly based in the United States, claim that 'a policy for safeguarding the environment is also a policy for safeguarding world peace' while, at the same time, starting and prosecuting an endless (and it is endless) series of wars which have resulted in the transfer of great wealth while at the same creating famine, starvation and genocide.

Ironically, the conspirators frequently claim that their actions have helped eradicate war. For example, they claim that the United Nations and the EU were both founded to stop war. This is patent nonsense. The world has more wars now than ever before. America has been at war almost constantly for 100 years. Never before, in human history, have as many people been killed or injured in wars as were killed or injured in the 20th century.

The bankers and their allies created the United Nations, an institution built on a fraud, to help them create a world government; and together with leftover Nazis they created the European Union, because they felt that regional powers would also lead them in that direction. And then they hurried things along by creating the climate change myth, regarding it and the absurdity of 'net zero' as effective weapons in their war for total control.

Finally, to hedge their bets, they continued with the war-making; inciting wars, deposing or killing unhelpful leaders and using loans and debts to enable them to steal natural resources.

We are witnessing the greatest crime in history and if we are going to do anything about it we have to recognise that time is running out.

Meanwhile, in order to fight this deadly virus of fear and lies, we need to follow the timeline and see who our enemies are, how they have fought this war. Only by doing this can we look at their

95

strengths and their weaknesses. In this part of the book I'm going to deal with the most significant influencers who have shaped our thinking on climate change, population control and other vital issues.

I should point out, of course, that the dates I have selected were taken not at random but as necessarily selective and representative of the clearly visible trend designed to take us towards a world government, using the pseudoscientific myth of climate change as the weapon with which to create fear, mass hysteria and compliance.

1762

Jean-Jacques Rousseau, a Swiss writer and philosopher, published The Social Contract in 1762. It was Rousseau who first pointed out that as people had grown less dependent on nature so they had become more dependent upon each other – with this, inevitably, leading to a loss of freedom. Today, we see this most vividly in the way that power cuts leave us helpless and strikers cause chaos. In 'The Social Contract', Rousseau pointed out that 'man is born free, and everywhere he is in chains' but then added that 'Those who think themselves the masters of others are indeed greater slaves than they.' Rousseau was an advocate of the 'back to nature' theory that is now so widespread. Curiously, however, he is now pretty well forgotten though he did have an influence as a very early environmentalist.

1798

This was the year when an English economist and vicar called Thomas Malthus created the notion that the earth could only hold so many people. He warned that population growth had gone faster than food production and that better living conditions meant that families were able to have more children. He also suggested that the increase in population was a result of a higher birth rate. All his theories were quickly proved to be quite daft. His first theory, that population growth would exceed food supply and cause starvation, has never been the case. There is a great deal of starvation in the world today (in 2023) but that is not because there isn't enough food but because there is too much food in some parts of the planet and not enough food in other parts. His theory that better living standards would mean more children has been proved wrong too. If anything, people usually tend to have smaller families as they grow wealthier. And his notion that the population was increasing because of a higher birth rate was also proved wrong. The population was increasing because more people were surviving infancy and, therefore, living longer.

Malthus's work led to the eugenics movement which suggested that undesirables and mentally ill folk should be sterilised to stop them breeding.

During the Third Reich, eugenics became very popular with the Nazis and the idea was spread around the world quite successfully by a number of people. For example, Margaret Sanger, a radical feminist and the founder of Planned Parenthood took the idea to America where she called for coercive sterilisation, mandatory segregation and rehabilitative concentration camps for all those she regarded as dysgenic. In the 1970s, George Bush (later to become President George Bush) said that 'it is quite clear that one of the major challenges of the 1970s…will be to curb the world's fertility'.

Today, those who promote the idea that the world is overpopulated (and that something must be done about it) are often rightly labelled as racist – a label which it is as difficult to remove as it is to deny. It is, I suspect, their insistence that the answer to the overpopulation problem lies with poor countries in Africa and Asia, rather than with billionaires with large families, that makes it easy for sensible observers to link the overpopulation argument with racism.

There are many large holes in the argument that the world is overpopulated and that there isn't enough food to go round. So, for example it is well established that farmers use less than half of the Earth's arable land and yet, despite that, global food production has consistently increased much faster than population growth. Moreover, some of the most populated countries on earth (such as the Netherlands) have nevertheless been traditional exporters of food.

Several food experts have suggested that the earth could easily support a population of 30-40 billion. Colin Clark of Oxford concluded that the earth could supply an American style diet for over 35 billion and that if people ate a Japanese diet, the earth could feed over 100 billion. Roger Revelle, the former director of the Harvard Center for Population studies, estimated that the earth could provide

2,500 calories a day for 40 billion people – even if farmers were using less than a quarter of the available land.

Finally, there is now a widely held belief that the problem is not that the earth is too crowded but that there are too few young people around. Many countries (including China and Japan) have tried to encourage couples to have more children.

1891

It was in 1891 that Cecil Rhodes, the man who first realised the extent of the mineral wealth in southern Africa (and who gave his name to a country), founded an organisation called The Round Table. Rhodes, who believed in the idea of a world government, also set up a fund for scholarships at Oxford University and many of the leading Americans for a century have been beneficiaries of that fund. Bill Clinton was just one famous Rhodes Scholar. The Round Table has steadily grown in influence over the years.

1913

US income tax was enacted in 1913 but within a few years, oil and mineral companies managed to free themselves from the onerous burden of paying taxes. They did this largely because they qualified for something called a US depletion allowance – which is a tax deductible credit reflecting the value of the oil which has been taken out of the ground. (Naturally none of this money goes to the countries from which the oil is actually being taken.) In addition, oil companies, like drug companies, manage to avoid paying tax by the use of foreign subsidiaries based in low or no tax countries. So, American oil companies took oil from Saudi Arabia and then sold it to Panamanian or Liberian affiliates. These affiliates then sold the oil to distributors in the US or Europe, making sure that the price was high enough to ensure that the distributors didn't have to pay much if any tax. Liberia and Panama are tax free zones and both use the US dollar as their currencies so they are extremely convenient.

1921

At the end of the Great War (later to be renamed World War I), American and British delegates at Versailles (where the Middle East was divided up and shared out among America, Britain and the major oil companies) formed something called the Institute of International Affairs and in 1921, the American branch of the Institute was created and named the Council on Foreign Relations (CFR). The Council's leadership and main influencers were bankers and lawyers acting for bankers. For over a century now the CFR has been at the centre of American politics and most Secretaries of State, National Security Advisors, CIA Directors and UN Ambassadors have been members. It has been usual, too, for chairmen of the Federal Reserve to be members of the CFR. Other members have included leading bankers. John Kenneth Galbraith and George F.Kennan (both of whom we will meet later) were also members of the CFR. It is the CFR not the two main political parties which controls the United States, and a fairly superficial scrutiny will show that The Republicans and the Democrats are actually members of the same party. (The same thing is true of the UK where there is rarely, if ever, any discernible policy difference between the three main political parties.) In his book *Power Shift*, author Alvin Toffler describes the people who have the power in the US as 'The Invisible Party'. In the UK, by the way, the British version of the CFR is known as the Royal Institute for International Affairs.

1930

The BIS was created in 1930 by the world's central banks, including the Federal Reserve Bank in New York and the Bank of England in London. The BIS was primarily the brainchild of Hjalmar Horace Greeley Schacht, the president of the German Reichsbank and the Nazi Minister of Economics.

Schacht set up the BIS because he knew that there was eventually going to be a war between Germany and other European countries. The plan was that the BIS would enable the Nazis to maintain channels of communication between Berlin and financial institutions around the world. Schacht made sure that the BIS's charter emphasised that the Bank would remain immune from censure or closure during war. Moreover, Schacht was clever enough to disguise the BIS's main purpose by claiming that the BIS would help Germany provide the Allies with financial reparations owed after World War I. However, instead of money flowing from Germany to the Allies, it went in the other direction and was used to help Hitler build up a war chest for the coming conflict. The Nazis were undoubtedly helped in this by the fact that the first presidents of the BIS, who were American, were easy to deal with. (One of the first presidents of the BIS was an American called Leon Fraser who had been a tabloid journalist and who had little or no background in banking.) The BIS, the central bank for central bankers, quickly became the most important and powerful bank in the world.

In March 1938, Hitler's armies moved into Austria, and one of the first things the troops did was to steal the nation's gold and transport it to vaults controlled by the BIS. More Nazi troops tried to do the same thing when they marched into Prague. Nazi soldiers demanded that the directors of the Czech National Bank hand over Czechoslovakia's supply of gold – $48 million worth. The directors replied that they had already moved the gold to the BIS with instructions that it be sent to the Bank of England. Unfazed by this, the Nazis simply instructed the Czechs to tell the Bank of England to send the gold back to Switzerland. The Governor of the Bank of England (a flamboyant and traitorous exhibitionist called Montagu Norman) made life easier for the Nazis by immediately authorising the BIS in Switzerland to take $48 million worth of gold from the Bank of England's account and to put it straight into the German account so that it was immediately available for the Nazis to use. By 1939, when the War began, the BIS had made many millions available to the Nazis.

For decades, the Bank for International Settlements, then and now the most powerful bank in the world, has been so secretive that it is not even mentioned in most books about the Second World War. Today, it is still the central bank for the world's central banks but it is no exaggeration to say that without the BIS and IG Farben there would have been no Second World War. And there would be no European Union.

In 1940 an American, Thomas McKittrick, was appointed president of BIS as a replacement for Leon Fraser. McKittrick was a lawyer and a friend of the Nazi party and he turned BIS into an arm of the Reichsbank. Fluent in German, McKittrick had previously worked for Lee, Higginson and Company and had made large loans to the Nazis. There is no doubt that McKittrick's sympathies were with Germany. Indeed, in 1940, during the War, he went to Berlin and had a meeting at the Reichsbank with the Gestapo. And the BIS under McKittrick continued to act as a middleman for stolen gold.

By the start of World War II, the BIS was already controlled by Hitler. McKittrick was the president of the Bank but the other directors included Hitler's economics adviser, Dr Walther Funk, Emil Puhl, a director of the Reichsbank, Hermann Schmitz, the head of the Nazi conglomerate known as IG Farben (the company which built the concentration camps and supplied the poison gas for the gas chambers) and Baron Kurt von Schroder, a banker and Gestapo officer.

Throughout the War, the BIS accepted and stored looted gold and carried out foreign exchange deals on behalf of Hitler. Much of the gold accepted by the BIS came from the teeth and belongings of concentration camp victims. Hitler's economics adviser, Walther Funk, worked with Heinrich Himmler (a leading Nazi and head of the SS) to ensure that gold from concentration camp victims was put into a special Reichsbank account. Gold from jewels, spectacle frames, watches, cigarette cases and teeth was melted down into 20 kilogram bars and sent to Switzerland where it could be 'laundered' through the Swiss National Bank before being made available to the Nazis, via the BIS, as 'clean' gold. McKittrick, who constantly provided the Reichsbank with intelligence material, helped the Nazis take control of occupied countries and their banks.

Astonishingly, the Bank of England continued to cooperate with the BIS throughout the War, although the British directors Sir Otto Niemeyer and Montagu Norman must have known that the BIS was effectively Hitler's inexhaustible piggy bank. Without the BIS's cooperation, the Nazis would have run out of money for arms and the Second World War would have probably never started or would have ended within a year or so at most. In June 1940, $228 million worth of gold which the Belgian Government was trying to send to safety was intercepted by the BIS and redirected to the Reichsbank. Money stolen from Holland also went via the BIS to the Nazis. Most of the money paid out by the BIS in dividends went to Hitler's Germany.

In February 1942, two months after Pearl Harbour, the Reichsbank and the German and Italian Governments decided that McKittrick should remain President of the BIS for the duration of the War. In one Nazi document it was stated that 'McKittrick's opinions are safely known to us'. The faith of the Nazis was well placed, for the BIS continued to provide gold for their use.

Throughout the Second World War, McKittrick travelled around Europe quite freely, on occasion being escorted by Himmler's special SS police force. McKittrick even went back to America for a meeting with the Federal Reserve Bank and then returned to Berlin where he reported to the Reichsbank.

Not everyone ignored what was happening in Switzerland. In his book *The Hidden Enemy*, published in 1943, Heinz Pol wrote: 'The Bank for International Settlements in neutral Basel, Switzerland, has been, since 1941, almost entirely controlled by Axis representatives...' In 1943, Congressman Jerry Voorhis of California called for an investigation into the BIS, demanding to know why an American was the President of a bank which was being used by and for the Nazis. Nothing happened. Again, in early 1944, Congressman John F Coffee asked similar questions. He pointed out that the majority of the board of the BIS was made up of Nazi officials but that American money was being deposited in the bank. At an International Monetary Conference held at Bretton Woods in 1944, a Norwegian economist called William Keilhau called for the BIS to be dissolved and for there to be an investigation of the bank's books and records. However, Keynes, an influential economist, said that the BIS should be allowed to continue until a new world bank and an international monetary fund could be set up. Amazingly, the argument for retaining the BIS was that the bank would help restore and rebuild Germany at the end of the War. It was argued that if the BIS were dissolved, the Germans would fear that their relationship with America might not survive the end of the War.

Nevertheless it was decided by the Americans that the BIS should be liquidated. Astonishingly, however, McKittrick simply refused to accept the decision. He wrote to America and to Britain arguing that when the War ended the Allies would have to pay huge sums of money for the rebuilding of Germany and that these would be best paid through the BIS. When questioned about the gold which the Nazis had stolen, McKittrick replied, apparently with a straight face, that it was being held in the vaults of the Reichsbank so that it could be returned to its owners after the end of the War. In May of 1944, McKittrick and his staff dealt with the $378 million in gold which the Nazi Government sent to Switzerland for use after the War. By then the Nazis realised that they were losing the War and the gold (some of which had been stolen from the national banks of Austria, Belgium, Czechoslovakia and Holland and some of which had been melted down from gold collected from jewellery, spectacle frames and teeth of murdered prisoners in the concentration camps) was intended to be used by the Nazis after the end of the War. McKittrick must have known this but he and the BIS were happy to deal with the stolen gold. In 1948, the BIS was ordered to hand the looted gold over to the Allies. The amount handed over came to just $4 million.

No one at the BIS ever admitted what had happened to the hundreds of millions in stolen gold which had been deposited there by the Nazis. No one ever found the $374 million which was missing from the money sent for the use of the Nazis after the end of the War.

There was ample evidence to show that McKitrick had willingly cooperated with the Nazis but after the War he was given important posts in America including being made vice-president of the Chase National Bank. (This was perhaps not surprising since during the War the Chase Bank in Paris had helped finance the Nazis.)

After the end of the War, Karl Blessing, a Nazi who had controlled an army of slave labourers in Germany's concentration camps, returned to the BIS and became president of the Bundesbank. Nevertheless, it was felt that someone from the BIS needed to be punished and so in 1945, Emil Puhl, who had been vice president of the Reichsbank and a director of the BIS, was one of the few civilian Nazis to be found guilty of war crimes. Puhl had been responsible for moving Nazi gold during the War – knowing that much of the gold had come from prisoners in Germany's various concentration camps. Puhl was sentenced to a modest five years in prison but he appears to have served very little of this and in 1950 he was invited by his friend Thomas McKittrick to visit America as his guest. Puhl, a Nazi economist, director of the BIS and the Reichsbank had been McKittrick's go between with the Nazis.

The Americans and the British wanted the Bank for International Settlements to be dissolved after the end of the War but instead, it went from strength to strength. In 1954, the European Coal and Steel Community (the forerunner of the European Union) asked the United States for a loan of $100 million. Inevitably, the loan was arranged with the help of the BIS – the bank which had worked closely with the Nazis during World War II.

Legally untouchable and existing outside all jurisdictions, the BIS was created to act as the central bank for central bankers. It is disturbing to realise that the BIS is still the most powerful financial institution in the world though many politicians, economists and bankers have never even heard of it.

The BIS has been at the centre of financial events since the end of World War II.

1941

In many ways, 1941 was the most significant year of the Second World War. It was in 1941 that the Allies began to put time and effort into post war planning. Roosevelt produced his 'Four Freedoms in January 1941, and the Anglo-American Atlantic Charter was published in that year. It was also in that year (after the Japanese attack on Pearl Harbour – which actually came as no surprise to anyone) that Roosevelt produced his draft for the public Declaration of the United Nations. Preparatory work was done by Alger Hiss who was a communist and a Soviet spy as well being a member of the Council on Foreign Relations. The document declared that the 26 states which had signed were fighting 'to defend life, liberty, independence, and religious freedom and to preserve human rights and justice in their own lands as in other lands'. The document was finally published on 1st January 1942 with the four great powers (the United States of America, the United Kingdom, the Soviet Union and China) listed first and 22 lesser states listed in alphabetical order. De Gaullist France was excluded from the list so as not to recognise it as a government.

And thus was born the United Nations, and, ironically, the beginning of the end of life, liberty, independence and religious freedom.

The United States had refused to join the League of Nations after World War I because it wasn't allowed to have veto power over decisions (the US has always refused to join any judicial, economic or diplomatic institution unless it has veto power) and the US only agreed to join the UN on condition that it had the power of veto. (And, of course, the US has veto power over the World Bank and the

International Monetary Fund – which effectively means that America controls these institutions.)

Because the US has veto power, the United Nations cannot punish American war crimes (the use of Agent Orange in Vietnam or the use of depleted uranium in Iraq and Afghanistan for example) and cannot punish America for the theft of land, gold and resources or the breaking of promises. (President Putin has described America as 'non-agreement-capable'.)

Today, America creates sanctions against other countries for no other reason than that the country being sanctioned has a policy which doesn't match American views. So, for example, the US has introduced sanctions against Uganda because it doesn't approve of Uganda's policy on lesbians and gays, etc.

1943

It is generally thought that American helped Britain win the Second World War by providing ships, fuel, food and so on. But things weren't quite that simple. The provision of arms and other help was a lend-lease scheme. In 1943, President Truman said: 'If Britain cannot pay us dollars for petroleum needed by her and cannot, by reason of a shipping shortage or other situation, procure the petroleum she needs from the petroleum she controls in Asia, South America and the Dutch East Indies, consideration should be given as to whether she might not pay for the petroleum obtained from us by transferring to us her ownership of an equivalent value of foreign petroleum reserves or of the English held securities of the corporations having title to such reserves.'

And that is what happened.

During the Second World War, the US opened up Britain and its Empire with a 'your money or your life' offer – knowing that Britain was desperately in need. By 1945, the US claimed $20 billion from Britain – leaving Britain close to being bankrupt. It seems that American politicians (or at least some of them) have never been able to forget or forgive the fact that their country was once one of Britain's colonies.

The US insisted that Britain join the International Monetary Fund (on America's terms) and demanded access to Britain's foreign markets. The terms of the loan which had helped Britain during the

War stopped Britain devaluing sterling until 1949, and that forced Britain's balance of payments into deficit. Sterling became a satellite currency of the American dollar.

What happened to Britain during and after the Second World War has happened to many other countries around the world. Loans are used to take control of assets and the bankers are the only winners.

America was the big winner in World War II, Germany did very well financially and Britain was the big loser.

1944

At the Bretton Woods Conference in 1944, two thoroughly evil financial organisations were set up: the World Bank and the International Monetary Fund. The two organisations were set up by a couple of deeply unpleasant men: Harry Dexter White (a communist and almost certainly a Russian spy) and John Maynard Keynes (a British economist who believed that governments could and should spend money they didn't have).

The first president of the World Bank was a Nazi lover called John McCloy. In her book *The Shocking History of the EU*, Zina Cohen explains that McCloy was the banker who helped war criminals (who had made huge amounts of money out of concentration camp slave labour) to avoid unpleasantness at the end of the War. McCloy also helped set up the United Nations and was, without a doubt, one of the nastiest villains of the 20th century.

Both these organisations are based in Washington.

The president of the World Bank is elected and somehow always manages to be American. As I write, the President of the World Bank is Ajay Banga who was previously head of Mastercard.

So that things don't look bad, the president of the IMF is not usually an American but that doesn't make any difference to anything. Both organisations are effectively controlled by and for American banks and financiers and whatever it might say in their constitutions, their real aims are to ensure that really, horrible rich people get even richer (for doing absolutely nothing of value) while poor people around the world (and poor and middle class people in America and Europe) struggle, work hard, get poorer and die as soon as they have stopped doing useful work. That's the plan and it's working out very nicely. The World Bank is officially two banks (the International Bank for Reconstruction and Development and the

106

International Development Association) and three other organisations. But the conglomerate is known as the World Bank.

Since the World Bank was created, the US policy has been to secure foreign markets for farmers and for industry. Grains and meat have long been an essential part of the US trade balance and both are used as weapons in the fight for global supremacy. US officials have led the World Bank to lend countries money for building ports, road building and other infrastructure and to promote the growing of crops such as palm oil, bananas, spices and rubber which don't compete with US farm products. Small farms go out of business as huge conglomerates take over the land. And, of course, the countries producing these products have to import (usually from America) the essential food supplies they need. Countries are pushed to hire US engineers and construction companies in order to produce these exports and they then see their earnings siphoned off with foreign owned companies (beholden to American banks) ending up with all the income. Local taxpayers are expected to pay back the cost of the construction work demanded by the US and facilitated by the World Bank.

The World Bank's policy of supporting large scale businesses (such as Monsanto-Bayer which is infamous for its policy of taking out patents on seeds which have been used by families for generations and thereby putting small farmers out of business) at the expense of small scale farmers has been widely criticised. It is, however, supported by the US Agency for International Development, the British, Dutch and Danish governments and the Gates Foundation.

1947

The globalists love creating new organisations designed to help create a world government. They obviously feel that having lots of organisations with the same aim means that their ambition will be more speedily fulfilled.

In 1947, the World Federalist Association was formed by a couple of members of the Council for Foreign Relations – Norman Cousins and James P.Warburg (a member of the family which had helped set up America's Federal Reserve System). The aim of the World Federalist Association is to turn the United Nations into a world government through a world court, a world income tax and an international peace force. (The United Nations describes its army as a Peacekeeping Force. Not everyone would agree with this name. UN troops helped a communist called Patrice Lumumba take over the Congo and slaughter innocent men, women and children in hospitals in the early 1960s.)

1949

NATO (the North Atlantic Treaty Organisation) was created in 1949 as a way to halt the spread of Soviet power in Europe. Today, NATO is pretty well controlled by the United States, with the other members doing what they are told. America is the big rock star and the other countries in NATO are session musicians providing backing music. NATO consists of dozens of committees and a huge military bureaucracy. In 2022, NATO backed Ukraine in its fight with Russia and created (for political reasons) a designer war. Ukraine was not (and is not) a member of NATO and there was no logical reason for NATO to be involved in the war. In the spring and summer of 2023, it was announced that NATO would send depleted uranium shells and cluster bombs to Ukraine to be used in the war. These actions turned all the leading politicians of the countries involved in NATO into war criminals.

1954

It is impossible to consider the plan for a world government without mentioning the Bilderbergers.

I have been writing about the Bilderbergers for decades, and like most other writers I've never been able to find out much about them. Although taxpayers around the world always pay for their security, the Bilderbergers and the Bilderberger delegates all keep their meetings very secret. And they naturally label as paranoid, and as conspiracy theorists, anyone who suggests that there might be something ever so slightly suspicious about a bunch of politicians, bankers, officials, intelligence agents, war criminals (I can name at least one war criminal who has attended), media tycoons and industrialists holding regular secret meetings to discuss the future of the world. Journalists who dare to try to find out what is going on, what the meetings are about and the names of the participants quickly find the meaning of the word 'secrecy'. The CIA and MI5 could take lessons in secrecy from the Bilderbergers.

You might think that having media tycoons at the Bilderberger meetings would mean that titbits of news might leak out occasionally. But you'd be very naïve to think that. Consider this quote from Bilderberger David Rockefeller: 'We are grateful to *The Washington Post*, the *New York Times*, *Time* magazine and other great publications whose directors have attended our meetings and respected their promise of discretion for almost forty years. It would have been impossible for us to develop our plan for the world if we had been subject to the bright lights of publicity during those years. But the world is now more sophisticated and prepared to march towards a world government. The super-national sovereignty of an intellectual elite and world bankers is surely preferable to the national auto-determination practised in past centuries.'

Named after the hotel where the conspirators first met in May 1954 (the Hotel de Bilderberg in Holland) the group was created by Prince Bernhard of the Netherlands, a powerful Dutch businessman, a friend of the Rothschilds and a former Nazi SS storm trooper who described his work for Hitler as a lot of fun and yet somehow managed to remain an eminent member of Dutch society after the end of World War II. Interestingly, Bernhard was a Nazi at the same time as Klaus Schwab's father. Schwab, of course, is the founder of the World Economic Forum. (The links between the Nazis and those who want a world government are never ending.) No attempt has ever been made to hide the fact that the intention of the Bilderbergers is to create a world government or as it has also been described a 'new world order'.

(As an aside, the Oxford Dictionary of English describes a conspiracy as a secret plan for a group to do something unlawful. Since the Bilderbergers are nothing if not secret, and since their plans do not have any legal authority but do impact on every citizen in the world, it is clear that the Bilderbergers are conspirators. (This fact rather weakens the labelling of those who write about them as 'conspiracy theorists'. The conspiracy is not a theory it is clearly a fact.)

Much is discussed at Bilderberg meetings, many decisions about our future are reached and many plans are put into action. There is much discussion of the usual issues such as world government, climate change, China, Russia, Brexit and the weaponisation of social media. The main aim is to create a one world government with one central currency and one bank and one army. However, although the decisions and the plans concern us all, the Bilderbergers insist on keeping all their deliberations quite secret. Nevertheless it is sometimes possible to trace events back to their meetings. For example, after one meeting (which was attended by Henry Kissinger, the U.S. President's advisor on foreign affairs) President Nixon opened up trade with China and devalued the dollar. Prince Bernhard had previously boasted that one of the subjects of Bilderberger meetings was to bring about 'change in the world-role of the United States'. There may be some who find it surprising that the American media, usually intensely patriotic and defensive, did not seem to mind one whit that an anonymous group of power brokers was intent on changing the world-role of the United States!

1959

The Council for Foreign Relations has controlled American foreign policy for many years. In 1959, the CFR published this statement: 'The US must strive to build a new international order which must respond to world aspirations for peace and for social and economic change.'

1962

It is generally believed that the World Wide Web was created by an Englishman, Tim Berners-Lee, but the internet was created some years before that.

American military experts were worried that one Soviet missile could destroy America's entire telephone system. An alternative was clearly required and in 1962, a scientist in America named J.C.R.Licklider proposed that a network of computers be set up that could talk to one another even if the telephone system was destroyed. In 1965, another scientist found a way to send information from one computer to another using a system called 'packet switching'. In 1969, the first message was sent from one computer to another. Each computer was the size of a small house.

During the 1970s, the network grew and by the end of the decade a large number of computers were involved.

And then in 1991, Tim Berners-Lee, who was working in Switzerland, introduced the World Wide Web. Instead of being used as a mailing system, the World Wide Web could be used to store information that anyone could retrieve. So Berners-Lee created what we now think of as the 'internet'.

And in 1992, Congress in the US, decided that the Web could be used for commercial purposes. (For the record that was the year when I first had a presence on the internet.) America has effectively controlled the internet ever since then. Without the internet, it would have been impossible for the conspirators to develop effective social credit systems or digital currencies.

We are constantly encouraged to believe that the internet has made the world a better place. But has it? It has taken away our freedom and created new stresses and pressures for everyone. Social media and social credit have taken us, with quiet certainty, towards the quiet death of the spirit. And surely it was easier to find a workman, for example, when you could look up local tradesmen in the telephone directory instead of having to plough through pages of misleading advertising and trying to decide which of the companies on the internet are genuinely offering a local service.

More importantly, the conspirators love the internet. It gives them complete control. It has removed all our privacy. All the major internet companies (Microsoft, Yahoo, Google, Facebook, YouTube, Skype, Apple, etc., etc.) will give your data to whichever government asks for it. Governments everywhere can see all your emails, chats, all your videos, all your pictures, all your contacts and all the websites you have visited. This intrusion began when Obama was President of the US (he gave government officials the right to monitor compliance and obedience and initiated the basis of social credit schemes in the US) and it has gradually become more intense. Governments claim that they have to look at what people are saying to help them deal with national emergencies such as the fake climate emergency which will always do very nicely, thank you, when any government department is looking for an excuse to do something intrusive. Since May 2023, the Federal Reserve in the US has been able to track everything you do with your money, and President Biden has been pushing for the IRS to be able to monitor everyone's bank accounts. Today, governments all around the world have established blueprints for controlling all their citizens and they are going to centralise everything, control all payment systems and give themselves the power to control how you earn, save and spend your money. All thanks to the internet. (In Canada, Trudeau used the 1988 Emergencies Act to freeze 266 bank accounts belonging to Canadians who had donated money to help the truckers protesting about mandatory vaccinations. Bank accounts of American citizens were frozen too.)

Without the internet there would be no social credit system. The internet has, indeed, been essential to the fraud that is the Great Reset. Allowing and encouraging anonymous comments and reviews was always difficult to understand until you realised how essential these have been for breaking down society, suppressing and demonising truth-tellers and destroying humanity. Governments everywhere have used their intelligence services to dominate the internet. In the US, the CIA has been dominant and in the UK the British army deployed its 77th Brigade to assist the security services MI5, Special Branch and GCHQ.

None of the things that has happened in recent years could have happened without the internet and there is no doubt that the internet has become the most powerful weapon against the people and against freedom. But things can get worse, much worse. If and when the authorities decide to insist that those using the internet have a digital licence to allow them access, the future will be bleak indeed for those denied such a licence. They will not be allowed to buy food or electricity. In June 2023, I reported that shoppers who wanted to buy food at an Aldi 'shop and go' store had to download an app before they were allowed into the store. Anyone without a smart phone and the Aldi app couldn't even enter the store. I wrote at the time that 'If we allow Aldi to get away with this then our war with the conspirators is over. We are well and truly inside the Great Reset. Anyone who shops at Aldi is a collaborator – aiding and abetting the totalitarian conspirators who want to take over our lives.' But few people took any notice or recognised the problem or thought about the millions of mainly elderly citizens who don't even own a smart phone. Thousands love the convenience of their smart phones and their ubiquitous apps.

Politicians, commentators and computer companies claim that the internet, smart phones and other developments have all improved life. But that depends on how you define 'improved'.

Are children better off playing games on computer consoles or spending hours every day keeping their Facebook profiles up to date and worrying about their social media ratings? Today's children feel delight when they receive an approving tick after re-posting a message written by someone else. Is that the new version of pride and self-satisfaction? (I have little doubt that the obsession with ratings on the internet is part of the plan to accustom us to a world in which we receive ratings for everything we do. The step from social media to social credit is a very small one.)

Social media has become so powerful that many now censor themselves for fear of being the victim of an organised attack by the mob (or, rather, the small number of woke collaborators who control social media) and losing their jobs, their money, their homes, and their reputations. There is no free speech and no debate. Social media has created a world in which people in cliques spend much of their time hurling abuse at one another. The world has become a series of factions – communists masquerading as liberals, transgendered individuals and their enthusiasts demanding ever expanding rights, gays demanding more of something, anything, black lives matter campaigners thinking up reasons to protest, pro-vaccine enthusiasts abusing those who question the safety and efficacy of vaccination programmes and so on.

And with internet robots, AI and government agencies adding to the smorgasbord of abuse, it is hardly surprising that in every country in the world fear has become the plat du jour. Mobile phones have, for many children, replaced friendships, family and schoolwork. Young people no longer live their lives in a natural way. They appear selfish, entitled and demanding and they overshare because they are constantly performing. They live in dread of the thumbs down buttons, the anonymous abuse, the disapproval from those within or without their tribe. Social media sites offer fame and fortune to the tiny few, and destruction and despair to the many. Dishonesty and hysteria are deliberately encouraged. Loaded weapons in their hands would do less harm than smart phones. Facebook alone has three billion users (I've never even been allowed onto the site for I was told that I was too dangerous to their community to be allowed to join). The lockdowns, the social distancing and the mask wearing regulations broke their spirit. In countries around the world clinical depression is now endemic among teenagers and undergraduates. Fears are created and exaggerated on a daily basis. Self-harm and suicide are endemic too. Research shows that children who spend a quarter of their waking hours staring at their smart phones (an average sort of level of obsession) do not develop mentally. Mask wearing slowed development still further. The combination of smart phones, lockdowns, social distancing and masks has caused anxiety, depression and aggression. Boys tend to watch violent video games and become aggressive. Girls tend to watch fashion videos on TikTok and their ambitions revolve around that and similar channels. It is not surprising that at school they absorb the garbage they are fed about climate change and blame the coming catastrophe on their elders. All this is being micromanaged by the collaborators on behalf of the conspirators. It is behaviour therapy designed to create anger and illness. Schools now dish out iPads in preference to text books and exercise books, though there is as big a need for health warnings on iPads as there is for warnings on cigarette packets. Such online legislation as exists is designed not to protect the innocent and vulnerable and naïve but to crush free speech and truth telling which is considered dangerous.

1967
The authorship of the Report from Iron Mountain has always been hidden behind the pseudonym 'John Doe' but there is no doubt that the Iron Mountain report is entirely genuine. (The establishment and the mainstream media have long argued that it is fake, and controlled opposition who have infiltrated the alternative or independent media have, for obvious reasons, also tried to dismiss the Iron Mountain report.) However, John Kenneth Galbraith, the Harvard economist and a long-term member of the establishment confirmed that the report was genuine and admitted that he was involved in its preparation. In the Iron Mountain Report, Galbraith and his colleagues explained that war, or the threat of war, was a good thing from the point of view of governments because it helped to convince the people of their right to rule. They also admitted that war allowed for more expenditure (on arms) and helped create a more stable political structure.

And when they looked for a substitute for war (or, rather, an 'add-on') Galbraith and his colleagues agreed that: 'the substitute... unless it provides a believable life-and-death threat it will not serve the socially organising function of war.'

The writers of the Special Study Group (who produced the Iron Mountain Report) also noted that: 'Economic surrogates for war must meet two principal criteria. They must be 'wasteful', in the common sense of the word, and they must operate outside the normal supply-demand system. A corollary that should be obvious is that the magnitude of the waste must be sufficient to meet the needs of a particular society. An economy as advanced and complex as our own requires the planned average destruction of not less than 10% of gross national product...'

The Special Study Group examined a number of substitutes for a traditional war, and considered a war on poverty and 'the threat of an out-of-our world invasion threat' and their report includes these words: 'It may be, for instance, that gross pollution of the environment can eventually replace the possibility of mass destruction by nuclear weapons as the principal apparent threat to the survival of the species. Poisoning of the air, and of the principal sources of food and water supply, is already well advanced, and at first glance would seem promising in this respect; it constitutes a threat that can be dealt with only through social organisation and political power. But from present indications it will be a generation to a generation and a half before environmental pollution, however severe, will be sufficiently menacing, on a global scale, to offer a possible basis for a solution.'

In a section entitled 'Substitutes for the Functions of War' Galbraith and his colleagues concluded: 'However unlikely some of the possible alternate enemies we have mentioned may seem, we must emphasize that one must be found, of credible quality and magnitude, if a transition to peace is ever to come about without social disintegration.'

And they add: 'It is more probable, in our judgement, that such a threat will have to be invented, rather than developed' and, in summary, note that 'what is involved here, in a sense, is the quest for William James' 'moral equivalent of war'.

Finally, the report's author gave readers some background information. He wrote: 'The general idea...for this kind of study dates back at least to 1961. It started with some of the new people who came in with the Kennedy Administration, mostly, I think with McNamara, Bundy, and Rusk.'

The enthusiasm for war (or some substitute) as a means of controlling the population has been espoused by other groups.

In their book, *Illuminati Agenda 21*, Dean and Jill Henderson report that in 1909, the trustees of the Andrew Carnegie Foundation for International Peace concluded: 'There are no known means more efficient than war, assuming the objective is altering the life of an entire people...How do we involve the United States in a war?'

1968

The Club of Rome was founded in 1969. It is described as a global think tank, and although it is without doubt global and doubtless a tank there doesn't seem to be much 'think' involved. The club follows the thinking of Malthus, and produced a report entitled *The Limits to Growth* which dealt with the rapidly growing world population and the allegedly finite resource supplies.

Members of the Club of Rome, who believe in sustainability and have links to the WEF, have claimed that the planet earth can only provide resources for one billion people, and so over six billion must die. Representatives of the Club have given many lectures and been given many awards for their work on overpopulation and climate change – both of which members seem to believe are real problems.

The Club of Rome has a sister organisation the Club of Madrid which, you will surprised to hear, supports sustainability and global governance. Members include Bill Clinton, Gordon Brown, a vast number of other former presidents and prime ministers and UN Secretary General Antonio Guterres.

1968

Reducing the world's population had been a popular theme among the globalists for some years but it was in 1968 that the argument about the world being crowded first became a popular topic in the media. That was when Paul Ehrlich published his sensational book *The Population Bomb* in which he warned that the world was vastly overpopulated. Ehrlich had obtained a doctorate after studying parasitic mites and the book was originally published by the Sierra

Club with Ballantine Books.

Ehrlich was always happy to offer journalists a prediction or two.

In 1967, writing in a British magazine called *New Scientist*, Ehrlich warned that the 'battle to feed humanity is over; and predicted that between 1970 and 1985, the world would undergo vast famines. He recommended putting luxury taxes on baby foods and diapers in order to discourage people from having babies, and advocated tying food aid in developing countries to population control.

Ehrlich got masses of publicity and helped found Zero Population Growth which advocated legalised abortion, government supported birth control, tax incentives for smaller families and a limit of two children per family (as was introduced in China). He argued that if population growth were maintained at its then rate, there would be 60 million billion people on earth within 900 years – with 100 people for every square foot of land and sea surface. His prediction took absolutely no account of famines, disease and so on. He said that the world's population would continue to grow as long as the birth rate exceeded the death rate and offered two solutions: finding a way to lower the birth rate or raising the death rate (through war, famine or pestilence).

Today, the conspirators still claim that it is necessary to reduce the size of the global population, and governments everywhere claim they are concerned not just by the size of their ageing populations but also by the overall size of their populations. And so there are global plans to cut the overall world population down from its current figure of around eight billion to a much lower number. The figure of 500 million (just half a billion) is widely quoted as the number of people that the earth can comfortably hold. This implies somehow getting rid of seven and a half billion people. All of this is based on a baseless tower of lies. Planet earth is perfectly capable of providing more than enough food for eight, ten or twelve billion people or even more and although there are clearly pockets of overcrowding, it is difficult to accept that the world is over-crowded. The certainty is that much of the food is in the wrong place at the wrong time (because of politics, greed and faulty logistics) and many people are also encouraged to crowd into huge cities when there would be plenty of room for them if they were allowed or encouraged to live in or around smaller communities.

It seems to me that the conspirators have two fundamental depopulation policies: 'End global poverty by killing all the poor people' and 'End disease by killing all the sick.'

Their whole cruel philosophy is actually based on a myth.

As I pointed out earlier, it was Thomas Malthus who, in 1798, first suggested that the world's population was growing too large and that the Earth's resources wouldn't be able to cope. Gloomily, Malthus predicted starvation, misery and war.

But the evidence shows that Malthus was wrong. The world population was two billion a century ago and today it is eight billion but the proportion of people living in abject poverty has fallen from 90% to 10%.

The irony is that if anything, the problem is that the population is growing too slowly. Population growth has slowed rapidly in the last half a century and in western countries in particular the percentage of elderly and dependent citizens has risen rapidly as a proportion of the total population.

There are, in short, too few working age citizens around. The result is that governments are introducing policies ruthlessly designed to kill off the elderly and the sick (in other words the 'dependent'). And the situation is getting worse. Governments and councils are committed to paying pensions that they cannot possibly ever pay. It is still not widely appreciated but pensions are not paid out of the taxes paid by those workers but by the taxes paid by the generation currently working. This has never before caused serious problems but today's younger generation seems to have taken exception to the way things work and have developed an antipathy towards the elderly which I find rather sad.

I first warned about this huge demographic problem in my book *Health Scandal* which was published in 1988 and recently republished.

1969

In 1969, Dr Jose M.R.Delgado published a book called *Physical Control of the Mind: Toward a Psychocivilised Society*. The book is as terrifying as the title suggests but Delgado has become increasingly significant in recent years with his work enjoying something of a renaissance.

This is what I wrote about his work in my book *Paper Doctors* in 1976:

'In the 1950s, Dr Delgado of the Yale University School of Medicine showed that two cats, normally quite friendly, could be made to fight fiercely if electrodes implanted in the brain were given impulses. Even when it continually lost its fights, the smaller of the two cats continued to be aggressive when stimulated. In one dramatic experiment, Dr Delgado wired a bull with electrodes and then planted himself in the middle of a bullring with a cape and a small radio transmitter. The bull charged but was stopped by Dr Delgado pressing a button on his transmitter. The bull screeched to a halt inches away from its target. Dr Delgado has reported that 'Animals with implanted electrodes in their brains have been made to perform a variety of responses with predictable reliability as if they were electronic toys under human control.'

Similar experiments have been performed with human beings. The patients selected had all proved dangerous and had shown that they had uncontrollable tempers. By electronic stimulation every patient was controlled. More detailed accounts of these experiments can be read in *Physical Control of the Mind* by J.M.R. Delgado.'

Delgado claimed that it was possible to control human behaviour in a number of ways:

By implanting electrodes deep in the brain of mental patients and preventing or provoking certain kinds of behaviour by stimulating brain centres with tiny electric charges.

Implanting tiny tubes in the brain and releasing into them drugs which change the activity of brain centres and hence behaviour.

Having a direct line of communication from a brain to a computer and back to the brain without having information pass through the sense organs.

Delgado reported that it was possible to control behaviour secretly because there are no visible wires or electrodes. Day and night supervision is possible without even touching the individual.

And thus was born, over 50 years ago, the idea of taking complete control the behaviour of human beings.

1970

In April of 1970, US President Richard Nixon announced the first

119

Earth Day and that same year he established the Environmental Protection Agency.

The then UN Secretary General, U Thant, was one of the first of many to offer a scaremongering prediction when he wrote that: 'For the first time in the history of mankind, there is arising a crisis of worldwide proportions involving developed and developing countries alike – the crisis of human environment…it is becoming apparent that if current trends continue, the future of life on earth could be endangered.'

Since Thant issued this warning, pretty much the same warning has been issued by every political leader, every media commentator and a Swedish schoolgirl.

And in that same month in 1970, an article by George F. Kennan appeared in the journal *Foreign Affairs* (the quarterly publication of the Council on Foreign Relations). Kennan argued that the 'war' on pollution would have to be international since 'the ecology of the planet is not arranged in national compartments' and that 'since this is an area in which no sovereign government can make these determinations, some international authority must ultimately do so.'

We were, in 1970, clearly heading towards some form of world government, and Kennan, the father of the Cold War between the US and the USSR, suggested a multilateral treaty or convention with an instrument of enforcement managed by 'true international servants' with 'dedication to the work at hand'.

Sadly, Nixon's scheme was not regarded as a huge success for two decades after Earth Day had been founded, one of the originators, Dennis Hayes, commented that 'Twenty years after Earth Day, those of us who set out to change the world are poised on the threshold of utter failure.' And Ken Weiner, who was Jimmy Carter's Deputy Director of the Council for Environmental Quality said: 'It has been said war is too important to be left to the generals. Some are wondering if environmental quality is too important to be left to the environmentalists.'

Not that this mattered much.

The seeds had been planted. And we were moving steadily towards the Great Reset.

1971

By 1971, America was spending so much on its military adventures that Nixon abandoned the link between gold and the US dollar. Prior to this date, countries had been able to convert $35 worth of dollars into an ounce of gold. De-linking dollar from the gold opened the way for dollar hegemony. America became the world's banker. America could print dollars all day long and use them to buy anything it wanted.

The neoliberals have, since then, used the dollar ruthlessly; buying land, minerals, public infrastructure, public companies, housing and goods with money they produced without restriction.

When America didn't need to hold enough gold to cover their dollars, the printing presses could run 24 hours a day. And eventually, of course, the Federal Reserve didn't even bother to have money printed. It just manufactured another few billion dollars out of thin air.

1971

1971 was also the year when a Professor B.F.Skinner published a book called *Beyond Freedom and Dignity*. (Dr Skinner's work on the book was paid for with a $283,000 grant from the US Government's National Institute of Mental Health.) Skinner, a social scientist, argued that if the world is to save any part of its resources for the future, it must reduce not only consumption but the number of consumers.'

The reviewer for *Time* magazine pointed out that Skinner's message was that 'we can no longer afford freedom, and so it must be replaced with control over man, his conduct and his culture. This thesis, proposed not by a writer of science fiction but by a man of science raises the spectre of a 1984 Orwellian society that might really come to pass'.

Skinner attacked individual freedom and dignity and predicted that Western culture might be replaced with the more disciplined culture of the Soviet Union or China. 'If you insist that individual rights are the 'summum bonum' then the whole structure of society falls down'.

The frightening thing is that Skinner's arguments and predictions were (and are) taken immensely seriously. And his work is now

121

revered by the globalists who want to reduce the world population by billions and to take total control of every aspect of our lives.

1971

The World Economic Forum (pompously and arrogantly announced as 'Committed to Improving the State of the World') was set up in 1971 by a man called Klaus Schwab, though the organisation wasn't called that then. When Schwab began what was to become the WEF he had an endowment of just 25,000 Swiss francs in a bank account.

The first Davos meeting of what was then called the European Management Symposium, lasted two weeks and involved 450 participants, including chief executives and senior managers from top companies and 50 faculty members from business schools.

Things then moved quickly.

The chairman of the second Davos meeting was supposed to be Herman J.Abs who had to cancel at the last minute but this link gives us a clear insight into the background of the WEF.

As Zina Cohen explains in her book *The Shocking History of the EU*, Abs was a bank director who helped Hitler enormously by forcibly purchasing Jewish banks at low prices. The money was then used to build the Nazi war machine.

During the Second World War, Abs was a member of a secret group formed in 1943 and known as the Committee for Foreign Economic Affairs – a group of bankers and businessmen who met to discuss Germany's future after the end of the War.

After the War, a friend of his, Charles Gunston of the Bank of England, asked Abs to help rebuild German banking – though Abs had been arrested as a war criminal and sentenced to death in his absence. Gunston worked for the Bank of England as the manager of the German desk and was a senior official in the British occupational authority after the War. Gunston cared nothing about the atrocities perpetrated by the Nazis. All he wanted to do was to help rebuild the German banks. To this end he recruited Abs who was high on a list of Nazi officials wanted for war crimes. Gunston protected Abs to help Germany rebuild its banking system ready to continue Hitler's work. Thanks to help from his friends at the Bank of England, Abs was not executed or even imprisoned, and by 1948, he was deputy head of the Reconstruction Loan Corporation and President of the

Bank Deutsche Lander. Unbelievably, it was then Abs who decided which German companies should receive the billions of dollars provided as Marshall Aid. And for decades afterwards, Abs had a powerful role in Germany. He was one of a number of former Nazis who helped create the organisation which became the European Union. (For more details of how the European Union was created please read 'The Shocking History of the EU' by Zina Cohen).

Until the mid-1990s, Abs was chairman of the Deutsche Bank and his Nazi background was ignored. *The Independent*, a British newspaper, described Abs as the outstanding German banker of his time and quietly ignored his work with IG Farben and Kontinental-Ol, where he had knowingly employed slave labour in the concentration camps. Nor did they mention the money he had helped steal from Jewish people and banks. And this was the man Schwab asked to chair the second Davos meeting of his new organisation. It has frequently been rumoured that Schwab's father was a Nazi who was an associate of Hitler but, of course, the fact checkers deny this.

The honorary sponsor of the third Davos meeting in 1973 was Prince Bernhard of the Netherlands (a former Nazi and the founder of the Bilderberger meetings) and the Commission of the European Communities 'renewed its patronage'. An Italian industrialist delivered a speech summarising *The Limits of Growth*, a book that had been commissioned by the Club of Rome and published in 1972. Participants drafted a code of ethics based on Klaus Schwab's stakeholder concept.

It was clear early on that the WEF was very close to the European Commission of the EU with two meetings held at the European Commission in Brussels.

Today, the WEF describes itself as a public interest not for profit organisation based in Switzerland. It has offices in New York (USA), San Francisco (USA), Tokyo (Japan), Mumbai (India) and Beijing (China). In 2022 the WEF reported an income of 383,000,000 Swiss francs in fees and other funding. Out of this 130 million Swiss francs was spent on staff, with Schwab himself reportedly being paid more than $1,000,000 a year (plus, allegedly, rewards from associated companies Around 252 million Swiss francs was spent on 'office and activity'. (It is interesting that many of those working with the conspirators in some way have become extraordinarily wealthy. Tony Blair, for example, was a modestly paid politician for most of his working life but is now a multi-millionaire. The staff of environmental and green charities are often enormously well-paid and enjoy first class travel around the world.) The WEF does not pay any federal taxes.

An organisation which, just a dozen years ago was regarded as having no influence and was known merely as the organiser of an annual shindig where virtue signalling celebrities such as pop star Bono (famous to many for his tax avoidance schemes and hypocrisy) could rub shoulders with politicians and industrialists eager to be photographed with famous people, and which was not taken seriously by many people, is now one of the most powerful bodies in the world. It has taken over from the far more secretive Bilderbergers as the face (and voice) of the conspirators.

Schwab himself was born in Germany in 1938 and acquired a variety of academic qualifications before founding the WEF in 1971 when he was just 33-years-old. The WEF was originally called the European Management Forum but changed its name to the rather grander and more ambitious World Economic Forum in 1987.

Just prior to founding the European Management Forum, Schwab had been a member of the Managing Board of a medium sized Swiss manufacturing company with which his father appears to have been associated. Today the WEF claims to have more than 600 employees but I would describe Schwab as (like Charles III and Tony Blair) as a fixer and a pimp for the conspirators. None of them seems to me to be serious players.

There is no record on the WEF's website of how Schwab acquired the money to set up what is described (on its own website) as 'the foremost global multi-stakeholder organisation' nor is it clear how, within three years, his organisation had been able to invite political leaders from around the world to a conference in Davos.

In 1971, the same year that he founded the forerunner of the WEF, Schwab wrote a book called *Modern Enterprise Management in Mechanical Engineering* (it seems unlikely that the royalties from this enabled him to found the WEF). There have been rumours that his mother was related to the Rothschild family and that his father was close to Adolf Hitler but both these suggestions have been dismissed by fact checkers (though we should remember that fact checkers claimed that the covid vaccine was effective and perfectly safe). In that early book, Schwab argued that the management of a modern enterprise must serve both the shareholders and the corporate stakeholders – with the stakeholders including employees, customers, government, creditors, local communities and financiers. Schwab has worked with the United Nations for many decades and has advised various UN bodies on sustainable development issues. Schwab has warned that there would be much anger in the world as the conspirators' plans unfolded, and is best known for warning citizens everywhere 'you will own nothing and be happy'.

As an aside, it is curious, is it not, how the phrase 'you will own nothing and be happy', which is believed to have originated with the World Economic Forum can be compared to the principles of the communist revolution as described in Karl Marx's 'Communist Manifesto'? Marx wrote that in order to establish a socialist dictatorship, and to obtain total control over the proletariat, the communists would have to eliminate all rights to private property, destroy all religion, which Marx famously described as 'the opiate of the people' and dissolve the family unit which was seen as a threat to the ability of the State to obtain total control over people's lives. (Today, under the Great Reset, traditional religions will be replaced by a faith in nature as defined by the United Nations and promoted by the consortium of bankers who are managing the global economy. Astonishingly, the leaders of traditional religions have accepted the change, and the Pope and the Archbishop of Canterbury seem happy to commit themselves and their followers to the pseudoscience in preference to the traditional teachings their religions have espoused. It doesn't seem to matter to them that the science of climate change is provably fake; they are wedded to, and happy to influence, the blasphemies promoted by the rabid environmentalists. In 2023, a WEF advisor and establishment enthusiast called Yuval Noah Harari claimed that AI could create a new religion and a new bible, thereby making AI the new god. This is, presumably, the proposed replacement for orthodox, traditional religion. We already know that AI will bring an endless encyclopaedia of lies to the internet, now, it seems, AI will also bring us a brand new fake religion.)

Actually, as Gary Allen and Larry Abraham point out in their excellent book *None Dare Call It Conspiracy*, which was published in 1971, the Communist Manifesto was merely an update of the revolutionary plans proposed 70 years earlier by Adam Weishaupt, the founder of the Order of Illuminati. Today we can see the WEF, the Bilderbergers and the other conspirators following the recommendations made by Marx, and previously by the Order of Illuminati.

Meetings of the WEF are held annually in Davos and participants arrive from all over the world (many of them in private jets) to discuss the threat of climate change.

Most dangerously, perhaps, the WEF has what it pompously calls a 'Young Global Leaders Scheme' which trains ruthless young men and women to be puppets of the cabal. Many of the graduates get jobs in politics, the green movement, charity management and so on, and Schwab boasts that 'graduates' from what might by some be seen as a brainwashing programme can be found in high places everywhere. The boast is justified and WEF followers can be found in many governments: Sunak in the UK, Trudeau in Canada and Macron in France all have links to the WEF.

The whole organisation reminds me very much of the Scientology cult though, as a replacement for the Bilderbergers and a promotional organisation for the European Union and the United Nations, it is infinitely more dangerous and it has influence far greater than would seem justified.

1972

The 1970s were a bad time for freedom, and the first meeting of the Trilateral Commission was organised in New York at the estate of David Rockefeller. All eight American representatives at the founding members were, unsurprisingly, members of the Council on Foreign Relations, and the purpose of the Trilateral Commission was officially stated as bringing together representatives from North America, Western Europe and Japan to improve the chances of a smooth and peaceful evolution of the global system. At least they didn't hide the purpose of the organisation.

David Rockefeller first floated the idea of the Trilateral Commission at a meeting of the Bilderberg Group where it proved extremely popular.

The formation of the Trilateral Commission had been foreseen by Zbigniew Brzezinski, President Jimmy Carter's National Security Chief who had argued that a world government would probably require two overlapping phases. Part one would involve the United

States, Western Europe and Japan forging a community with other advanced countries such as Israel, Mexico and Australia. Part two would extend the links to communist nations.

1972

The United Nations Educational, Scientific, and Cultural Organisation (UNESCO) set up the World Heritage Treaty in 1972. The WHT had a committee, of course, and listed procedures for listing cultural 'heritage' sites around the world. The WHT called for cooperation with 'international and national governmental and non-governmental organisations (NGOs'). As a result of this new organisation's formation, nations around the world suddenly reported that the official 'heritage' sites and local citizens were encouraged to believe that having an area designated a 'heritage site' was an honour to be cherished. Huge areas of land were designated 'heritage' sites with, for example, almost half of New Zealand's South Island being listed as a world heritage site. Huge tracts of land around the world are now so designated.

Once a piece of land is listed as a world heritage site, all local farmers, ranchers and loggers can be excluded, and all development must be stopped with UNESCO effectively acquiring ownership rights.

World heritage sites were set up as a first step towards re-wilding huge areas of the world.

1974

In an article entitled *The Hard Road to World Order* which appeared in *Foreign Affairs* (the house journal of the very powerful Council of Foreign Relations) Richard Gardner wrote that 'if instant world government, (UN) Charter review and a greatly strengthened International Court are not acceptable to the people, what hope for progress is there?'

Gardner suggested the following ways to get rid of national sovereignty: A reform of the international monetary system; a rewriting of the ground rules of international trade; subjecting all countries to international surveillance; a steady increase in the resources of agencies such as the World Bank, giving them more power over economic policies; continued strengthening of the global and regional authorities charged with protecting the world's environment; population policies designed to achieve zero population growth; a control of food supplies; a new international control of the world's oceans; new rules and institutions to regulate emerging communications technologies; a limit to conventional weapons and increasing use of UN forces to patrol and supervise.

1976

You might be surprised to hear that re-wilding is not a new concept. The World Wilderness Congress, which began in 1976 claims that it is the 'longest running, public environmental forum to build awareness and support for wilderness'. They claim to have initiated the process that led to the World Bank's Global Environmental Facility.

When the Fourth World Wilderness Congress met in 1987, delegates were probably delighted to find that the Denver Declaration for Worldwide Conservation had been prepared for them. The founder of the WWC announced that the declaration was the 'new Magna Carta'.

Within a few years, the American Congress had authorised spending over $1 billion a year on purchasing private taxpayers' property – and locking it away so that no one could waste it by building homes, farms, shops, schools, hospitals or factories on it. In just eleven American states there were already 86 million acres of wilderness and 133 million more acres were already designated for inclusion.

In Australia and Brazil, areas of land designated as suitable to be classified as 'wilderness' were measured in square miles. Over 12 billion acres of land was designated as wilderness areas.

It was at this Congress that it was revealed that United Nations agencies, aid agencies and private NGOs had put together a massive surveillance database called the 'World Wilderness Inventory'. The database had been put together by the Sierra Club (a private organisation which was founded in 1892 and is described as an 'environmental organisation').

Among those attending World Wilderness meetings have been David Rockefeller of Chase Manhattan bank and Baron Edmund de Rothschild of the Rothschild banking family.

And, you won't be surprised to hear that a World Conservation Bank was proposed to act as an intermediary between developing countries and private banks. Debts and loans would be cooked up and huge areas of land would be transferred to the World Conservation Bank. In other words, the World Conservation Bank would buy loans from developing countries and those countries would collateralise their loans with areas of land which could be designated as wilderness. If the debtor failed to meet their obligations, the WCB and its stockholders would end up owning vast areas of land together with the oil, minerals and other goodies underneath the land.

The world's biggest and most powerful bankers, the Establishment pushing for the New World Order, had been generous enough to find a 'green' way to take ownership of 30% of the world's uncultivated land mass. So, to give just one example, Madagascar's Government swapped thousands of acres of its own land for over $2 million worth of bad debt.

How wonderfully kind and unselfish of the bankers.

And how very simple.

You just get a country into debt (by lending them money they can't possibly pay back) and then you allow them to swap the debt for huge quantities of land – preferably wild land with lots of valuable goodies hidden underneath the surface.

Governments, NGOs, banks, Green political parties on the fringe of power and tax exempt foundations had come together to enable very rich and powerful people to take ownership of vast areas of the world's landmass.

Naturally, President Gorbachev of the USSR thought it a splendid idea. 'The Soviet Union favours a substantive discussion of ways to settle the debt crisis at multilateral forums,' he said 'including consultations under the auspices of the United Nations, among heads of governments of debtor and creditor countries.'

Are you now beginning to see how everything fits together?

Oh, and you may or may not have guessed that the people proposing that vast areas of land be classified as 'wilderness' (and not used for building or farming) just happen to be the same people who claim that the earth is vastly overpopulated.

And there's something else.

Do you remember the film *Goldfinger* in which the baddie (Mr Goldfinger) wanted to destroy the value of America's gold so that the value of HIS gold would soar in value? Well, you may see the similarity here with what the banks were planning. If they control wilderness areas which are rich in oil and minerals they don't have to do anything at all with the land to increase the value of their own holdings. It's the Goldfinger principle. By taking oil and minerals out of circulation the value of their own holdings will rocket.

1989

The New York Times (for many years a propaganda sheet for the globalists and conspirators) reported in 1989 that Margaret Thatcher (then the British Prime Minister)had warned that global warming could cause devastating floods and food shortages, though there was no evidence (scientific or otherwise) for this prediction. Mrs Thatcher called upon the United Nations to complete, by 1992, a treaty that would require action towards stabilising the world's climate and she told the General Assembly of the UN that the treaty should be supplemented by specific, binding agreements regulating the production of gases that trap heat in the atmosphere. Mrs Thatcher added that the restrictions would have to be 'obligatory and their applications carefully monitored'.

Mrs Thatcher was effectively repeating the strategy that had been outlined by George Kennan in an article which had appeared in the journal *Foreign Affairs* in 1970.

There was no evidence for the claim in 1970, there was no evidence for the claim in 1989 and there is no evidence for the claim now.

1990

The prediction that it would take a generation to a generation and a half for environmental pollution to be a useful weapon with which to scare the public appears to have been pretty accurate for in 1990, at a conference entitled 'Globe '90', the *Seattle Post-Intelligencer* reported that the former Norwegian prime Minister Gro Harlem Brundtland had told the audience that: 'Environmental destruction is a 'ticking time bomb' that poses a more absolute threat to human survival than nuclear annihilation during the Cold War'.

There was no evidence whatsoever for this absurd claim.

1991

The USSR fell apart in 1991 after America had won the Cold War. The year before that the World Bank and the IMF had laid out a plan to force Russia's leaders to impose austerity on their people and to give away the nation's assets. President Gorbachev naively trusted the US Government and accepted America's offer to help the Soviets privatise their economy so that money could be available to invest in the country.

President Bush promised Gorbachev that NATO would not move eastwards if Russia agreed to let East and West Germany integrate. However, when Clinton became President he reneged on the deal, broke America's promise and simply reminded Gorbachev that he didn't have a deal in writing. (Michael Hudson, in his book *Destiny of Civilisation* points out that breaking promises and treaties has been American policy since the nation's birth, 'as shown by its dozens of broken treaties with Native American tribes in the 19th century down to its withdrawal from the Joint Comprehensive Plan of Action with Iran in today's world'.)

The result of Gorbachev's action was that a favoured few Russian kleptocrats registered public assets in their own names, sold shares to foreign banks and became immensely rich overnight.

America became angry when President Putin ended the giveaways, and treated Mikhail Khodorkovsky as a hero for accumulating a fortune of $15 billion by buying privatisation vouchers and helping himself to oil reserves in Siberia. (Most of the other oligarchs moved to the West, bought huge properties, yachts and football clubs.)

Western investors who were in the know made billions by investing in the former public assets (including, inevitably, oil companies). Naturally, they paid no taxes.

National Security Advisor Brzezinski boasted that Russia had passed 'into de facto Western receivership'.

Gorbachev, the darling of the West, who had overseen this massive give away, didn't last long.

And when President Putin was democratically elected and tried to stop the foreign investors from helping themselves to his country's wealth (and then sending it abroad as dividends, interest and capital) the Americans were furious.

While the Warsaw bloc countries were weakened by what had happened, the United States (and their pet NATO) expanded. Officials reinforced their view that the US alone had the right to use nuclear weapons first and that the US alone had the right to use military force unilaterally. President Clinton's administration announced that it no longer felt bound by the UN Charter prohibiting the threat or use of force. And the US announced that it had the sole right to use force to ensure 'uninhibited access to key markets, energy supplies and strategic resources'.

(Neither Clinton nor anyone else in the White House seemed interested in the fact that international law defines such behaviour as 'aggression' and 'the supreme international crime'. That, at least, was the view of the judges at Nuremberg.)

The result was a new Cold War with the US and its NATO allies ranged against China and Russia and any countries resisting the theft, by the US, of their land and resources. Everywhere NATO went it left behind huge numbers of bodies, destroyed towns and countries with no future. But every time NATO went somewhere, American billionaire bankers got much richer.

1991

The Trilateral Commission published a book entitled: *Beyond Interdependence: The Meshing of the World's Economy and the Earth's Ecology* by a Canadian called Jim MacNeill who was general secretary of the World Commission on Environment and Development (which was also known as the Brundtland Commission). The book warned that the world was coming to an end and that there was a desperate need for a world government.

MacNeill argued that it should be at the Rio Earth Summit in 1992 that the Establishment should take on the responsibility for the future of mankind.

The foreword to the book was written by David Rockefeller who argued (with insider knowledge, of course) that 'environmental issues are rightly moving onto the central policy agenda and we all feel the need for a new synthesis'. (Sadly, there was no translation of what he meant in the book.)

The introduction was written by Maurice Strong who had been executive secretary of the first eco-summit 'The 1972 Stockholm Conference on Human Environment'. (If you are beginning to feel dizzy at the existence of so many organisations with the same general, grandiose purpose you are not alone.) Strong argued that decisions must be made that 'will literally determine the fate of the earth' and talked of an intermeshing of economic independence and ecological independence and an intermeshing of the two. (The one thing the ego warriors can do, other than hold up traffic and sprinkle coloured chalk dust in an irritating manner, is to create an impenetrable and instantly forgettable phrase or sentence. I feel bad about having to include so many of them in this book but if we are to follow the bits of bread in the forest we need to learn to read the runes. See what I mean?)

What MacNeill was talking about (in the code of the time) was international central planning, a more equitable distribution of wealth, the end of national sovereignty global control of resources, global central planning and a reduction in the global population. If you are beginning to think that this all sounds just a touch like something Karl Marx might have written then you are probably not alone. In practice, there is little or no difference between modern environmentalism, communism and, of course, fascism. They are, in practical terms, identical and interchangeable.

MacNeill warned about overpopulation, global warming, deforestation, bio-diversity, acid rain, rising sea levels and overpopulation and also talked about sustainable development and sustainable growth. There was talk of the Earth Summit involving representatives of most governments, hundreds of major industries and thousands of non-governmental organisations – all of course, with axes which needed sharpening – and he talked of the need for environmental taxes, probably to be administered by the United Nations. (Though the UN staff would probably remain untaxed.)

MacNeill demanded an Earth Council or World Environment and Development Forum to govern earth and look after the ordinary people who can no longer be trusted to have a say in how the world is run.

As usual, the only thing missing from this feast of rhetoric was the presence of any facts. There were many warnings and much tub thumping but not a lot else.

Sadly, Mr MacNeill is no longer with us though according to the Community Research Connections (which is, so it proudly says, a Sustainable Community Development) he was recipient of many honours, was Chairman of the World Bank's Independent Inspection Panel and he was a member of far too many panels and institutes and boards for me to list here without your eyes glazing over. Mr MacNeill is one of a new breed of professional advisors who travel the world, sitting on committees and panels and being well-paid to spread anxiety and incomprehensible solutions.

Before and after this meeting, President Gorbachev of the USSR published proposals which bore an uncanny resemblance to the proposals which were published in Rio. It's no surprise that as far as the West was concerned, Gorbachev was the most popular President of the USSR for many decades.

In *The New York Times* in December 1989, Gorbachev was reported to have spoken at the United Nations and said: 'International economy security is inconceivable unless related not only to the world's agreement but also the elimination of the threat to the world's environment…Let us also think about setting up within the framework of the United Nations a center for emergency environmental assistance.'

1992

In Rio de Janeiro in Brazil in 1992, the United Nations held a massive and now infamous shindig called UNCED which was designed to make environmentalism the world's most important topic. It was here that the UN's Earth Charter was born and it was here that the UN revealed (to a no doubt excited audience) its plan for the future called Agenda 21 – an 800-page detailed plan written to help the UN and its supporters take over the world and run everything in the name of 'sustainable development', with huge costs to be paid by unwitting and probably unwilling taxpayers everywhere.

There was also a Global Warming Convention and a Biodiversity Convention. The people at the UN (like all Greens) love treaties and conventions and declarations. And they love committees and meetings – especially if the meetings are held somewhere pleasant and the expenses are paid by someone else (preferably taxpayers).

The participants at UNCED were largely collaborators working for the conspirators. The conspirators themselves (the financiers and bankers who were behind the climate change fraud) usually prefer to stay behind the scenes, just pulling strings as and when they feel it is appropriate or necessary.

The plan was simple: to form more international institutions of control, to get governments to sign treaties on global warming and to designate the national and international agencies 'that will bear responsibility for the first phase of implementation, tentatively set for the last seven years of this century'. In other words the aim was to create instability and fear to unsettle the world's citizens.

It was generally agreed that the world was in a pretty rotten state and that it was possibly either getting too hot or too cold and that whatever was happening was all the fault of people who needed to be punished. This meeting in Rio was the culmination of the Iron Mountain shindig held a generation and a half earlier. The Iron Mountain predictions were bang on the button, though that wasn't much of a surprise.

With no hard evidence to support their position, the conspirators (and don't forget they founded the United Nations) chose climate change (and environmental problems in general) as a way to terrify populations everywhere, to excuse aggressive plans and to mobilise a growing army of collaborators who could be convinced to demonstrate and form action groups.

Since the financiers and conspirators controlled the mainstream media, it wasn't easy to manipulate the message being fed to viewers and readers everywhere around the world.

Greedy megalomaniacs had now forced governments everywhere to adopt long-range policies that were based more on science fiction than anything resembling real science. Liberal intellectuals, teachers and lecturers absorbed what they were fed and became enthusiastic purveyors of misinformation to their students.

The myth of climate change became integrated into school and college curricula. And the myth was accompanied by the convenient belief that the 'new' problem could only be solved by a combination of kindly, caring governments and determined and committed NGOs. A new industry was born with billions of dollars to spend on propaganda. Dozens of new foundations were founded, mostly led by key insiders and members of the establishment. The Sierra Club, the World Wilderness Congress, the Centre for Earth Resource Analysis, the Heritage Trust, the Nature Conservancy, the World Wildlife Fund and so on control billions of dollars and are all involved in spreading the same message.

There were plenty of lies and imaginative graphs and pie charts to excuse the plans for the world. But there was never any evidence.

Any teacher who tells children that global warming is real is guilty of a crime of unimaginable proportions and unimaginable consequences. This dangerous propaganda is nothing more than an unpleasant branch of science fiction and is destroying the lives of generations.

It is, of course, impossible to prove that there isn't any evidence to support the myth of climate change (nee global warming). But nor is there any evidence to support the lies which are so freely shared. And the most convincing proof that they are lying comes in the fact that climate change promoters will not debate their claims.

1993

Every time there is famine, flood, wildfire or any sort of 'natural' problem, anywhere in the world, the climate change cultists blame the weather. More specifically and more significantly, they blame man-made climate change.

But they are always lying.

Let me illustrate how and why they are lying with this very short discussion of what happened in Somalia in 1993, when the United Nations and the US Military launched 'Operation Restore Hope' to help a population officially devastated by drought, desertification and civil war.

What was not widely reported was that Somalia's problems began in the 1980s. Up until that time, Somalia had been pretty much self-sufficient in food. Then the IMF and the World Bank decided that Somalia needed help. And, as Ronald Reagan once said, the most dangerous and frightening words in the world are: 'I'm from the government and I'm here to help.'

The banks decided that Somalian agriculture needed reform and decided to help.

Before anyone knew what was happening, Somalia had huge, unpayable debts to Washington based financial institutions –

particularly the World Bank and the International Monetary Fund. Somalia had been helped into destruction.

Here's what really happened.

First, Somalia was told that it needed a 'structural adjustment programme'.

Within a short time, Somalia became dependent upon imported grain and in order to pay the bills for the imported grain the country had to borrow money.

The cheap imports with which Somalia was supplied by the kindly bankers meant that local farmers couldn't make any money. Farming communities became impoverished.

At the same time the best agricultural land was appropriated by people with links to the Government. This land was used for producing fruits, oil seeds and cotton which America wanted.

The Somalian currency then collapsed and the price of imported materials rose.

The World Bank decided that it could 'help' by insisting that farm animals should be vaccinated.

Naturally, the vaccines and the vets cost a good deal of money. The World Bank said that 'veterinarian services are essential for livestock development'. The Somalians had managed quite well without vaccines for a very long time. (The vaccine ploy has been used widely for many years and is now universal in the US, the EU, the UK and elsewhere. Farmers who do not have their animals vaccinated are not allowed to sell them. Even pet owners are forced to have their animals regularly vaccinated and micro-chipped.)

Water supplies were then taken over and privatised.

The local farmers, nomadic herdsmen couldn't cope and were decimated. The World Bank thought this was a good thing because nomadic farmers in sub-Saharan Africa were viewed as a cause of environmental degradation.

The Somalians could then not afford the vets or the vaccines and the result was that Somalian cattle exports plummeted. Their beef was not vaccinated and therefore not acceptable. Instead of buying Somalian beef, their customers bought from suppliers in Australian and the European Community.

The Somalian Government was put under strict controls by the IMF and tight budget targets were set by IMF 'experts'.

The banks then provided aid.

Unfortunately, the help wasn't provided as money or equipment but as food. The Government couldn't give the food to the people but had to sell the food in order to raise money to pay the foreign banks.

The outside banks then took control of the country.

The economic changes meant that health and education programmes collapsed. School enrolment collapsed, school buildings deteriorated, school materials could not be bought and then schools simply closed. And thanks to the intervention from the banks, wages collapsed by about 90%. The World Bank then took over the civil service. Public expenditure was tightened.

By 1989, Somalia had to find 194.6% of its export earnings to cover its debts. The country was effectively owned by the US controlled banks.

And when the people of Somalia started to starve to death because they weren't growing any food and couldn't afford to import any food, the US controlled IMF and World Bank very kindly stepped in with more aid and more loans and more debt.

Actually, of course, the money for those loans comes from Wall Street Banks. And it is the banks which hold the debts.

Within less than a decade and a half the US controlled banks had effectively taken ownership of Somalia and all its resources.

And naturally the owners of those banks, the conspirators who are pushing for a Great Reset and a World Government, blamed climate change.

Exactly the same thing has happened all over the world.

The American bankers use the power of the dollar and the world's agencies to exploit and steal. They overthrow any leaders who dare to stand up to them. They used armed force (provided by the American government) to install compliant dictators and then claim that the oligarchies they have created are evidence of westernised democracy. They force foreign countries to keep their central bank savings in the form of loans to the US Treasury so that none of their 'investments' costs them a penny.

American neoliberals working with and for the banks have mastered the art of turning public enterprises and honest, simple utilities into interest paying financial vehicles. And when they have created a large debt, they appropriate that country's land and resources and keep them for themselves. The American taxpayers underwrite the thievery but it is the American oligarchs who benefit. And this has been going on since the 1980s. Today, a tiny number of Americans (bankers, financiers and property dealers) now possess more wealth than the whole of the middle class.

The enthusiastic climate change nutters are merely aiding and abetting global genocide and the end of freedom and whatever remains of democracy.

If you don't believe that the US would do such things please do a little research of your own into precisely what happened in Somalia.

Or, indeed, in any other country which has been allegedly devastated by climate change.

And take a look, for example, at the way the IMF forced Thailand and South Korea to allow more foreign ownership of their economies and how, as a result, American companies ended up owning key sectors in those countries.

1994

In 1994, the United Nations Framework Convention on Climate Change came into being with the aim of preventing 'dangerous' human interference with the climate system. (This is odd wording since there are currently numerous attempts being made to interfere with the climate. So, for example, one enormously dangerous, even insane, plan is the one which involves spraying substances into the air in order to stop the sun's rays hitting earth.)

Today, most reputable scientists accept that manmade climate change is a myth and that the whole climate change movement is based on fraudulent evidence. Back in 1994, there wasn't even any fake evidence available. The UN created its Convention on Climate Change on little more than a whim. 'The objective was to stabilise greenhouse gas concentrations… to enable economic development to proceed in a sustainable manner.'

Countries which were deemed to have contributed most to the alleged problem were expected to reduce their emissions to 1990 levels though there was never any scientific evidence that this was practical or even a good idea.

The UNFCCC is one of three conventions brought into being at the Rio Earth Summit in 1992 (the other two were the UN Convention on Biological Diversity and the Convention to Combat

Desertification) and the UN reports (in its usual pompous and meaningless way) that it was 'in this context that the Joint Liaison Group was set up to boost cooperation among the three Conventions, with the ultimate aim of developing synergies in their activities on issues of mutual concern.'

The United Nations does not like to trouble itself with boring science or with dull evidence, and especially doesn't like to trouble itself with scientific facts; it prefers to concentrate on creating 'conventions', having very expensive conferences and forming liaison groups. The UN is all about laws and rhetoric and getting other people to do things.

2005

New Zealand, Chile, Brunei and Singapore created the Trans-Pacific Partnership in 2005. The partnership was a mutual trade agreement.

In 2008, the United States decided to take over the TPP and the Obama administration sponsored lobbyists to transform the TPP into an agreement designed to block the public regulation of health, the environment, or other public interest problems that might interfere with corporate profits – namely American corporate profits. Once again, Obama protected the big international companies and the bankers and punished the people who had been foolish enough to vote for him.

Obama's bailouts made the crooks ever richer and impoverished still further the poor and the middle classes. The destruction of the middle classes and the poor is a deliberate neoliberal policy, in the same way that the destruction of Third World economies is a deliberate policy.

The American version of the TPP gave power to a new court (an Investor State Dispute Settlement court) which could stop governments from suing companies and investors who had caused damage. Worse still, ISDS tribunals could order governments to pay fines to foreign companies which felt that public regulations had impaired their profits. The tribunals could order a government to pay a company any amount it liked, without limit. And so the new court made it possible for bankers and companies to do what they liked to a country without any penalty. And if a bank or company felt that a country's labour or safety regulations might damage its profits, it could sue the Government for loss of profits.

So, for example, when an Ecuadorian court ordered the oil firm Chevron to pay $9.5 billion in damages for causing pollution, an ISDS tribunal in The Hague overruled the Ecuadorian Supreme Court. To make matters worse the ISDS fined Ecuador $1.8 billion, plus interest, for cancelling a joint exploration venture with the oil giant Occidental.

Small countries are regularly ruined by these lawsuits which often involve small sums of money for the globalists but huge sums of money for the countries involved.

The US Chief Justice, John Roberts has said that ISDS has the power to review any nation's laws and annul the actions of that country's legislature, executive and judiciary.

The ISDS tribunals (which make the judgements) consist of three private sector lawyers who may also be the lawyers acting for the companies which have brought the legal action. So the three lawyers bring a lawsuit and then decide who wins. And then they decide how much money the country should pay, in dollars, for daring to violate American corporate rights.

It is, by any definition, nothing more than a racket and just as bad, if not worse, than anything conceived by the Cosa Nostra.

Bankers and companies can even sue for what they claim are potential future profits.

All this sounds like something out of a bizarre piece of fiction. But it isn't. It's all true.

Oh, and one other thing: all this pro-American legislation (much of it dealt with in secret) means that consumers have absolutely no way of knowing whether the food which they eat has been genetically modified, grown with hormones, treated with chemicals or anything else.

The conspirators behind all this can do what they damned well like. And no one can stop them.

And it is worth remembering that these laws were introduced by the Obama Administration which was ruthlessly pro-corporate. And nothing has changed. In 2021, President-elect Joe Biden wrote in *Foreign Affairs* magazine that his incoming 'foreign policy agenda will place the United States at the head of the table'.

Thanks to the neoliberals all international law is now drawn up by corporate lobbyists employed by the conspirators working towards the Great Reset.

2007

The American housing bubble, and subsequent financial collapse, didn't happen by accident. Banks deliberately pushed house prices to unsustainable levels and, in order to find a constant stream of 'greater fools' to keep buying overpriced properties, the banks offered 100% loans with no down payment. Hundreds of thousands of dollars were loaned to what were called NINJA buyers – they had no income, no job and no assets. Mortgages were given to unemployed black and Hispanic minority borrowers who had no way of paying back the interest. When the inevitable happened, President Obama (a long established 'insider') refused to prosecute the banks who falsified income statements and provided false property appraisals. Instead Obama bailed out the big banks with taxpayers' money – thereby making the bankers at the big institutions a great deal richer. The bankers used the huge loans they were given not to help their customers but to pay themselves huge and utterly unjustifiable bonuses. The losers were the millions of families and individuals who had trusted the banks. Many of them went bankrupt as their homes were taken from them. Home ownership fell as private equity companies set up by financiers bought foreclosed properties at distressed prices and then rented them out at huge profits. None of this could have happened without Obama, who was rewarding his Wall Street campaign contributors. The home owners were not allowed to have their mortgages written down to the 'distressed sale' prices. Only the banks benefited from the bailouts. The black and Hispanics who lost everything had been the major supporters of Obama in the Presidential elections. The 2007-8 housing collapse was a class war with racial and ethnic overtones. And Obama, the man millions had trusted, had shown himself to be on the side of the rich, white, mostly Jewish bankers. In his autobiography *A Promised Land* (for which he received a huge advance payment) Obama said he worried that 'stretching the definition of criminal statues to prosecute banking executives' would have 'required a violence to the social order'. Michael Hudson, the author of *Destiny of Civilisation* points out that: 'The refusal of President Obama and his Department of Justice to prosecute show the degree to which the distinction between rent-seeking and outright fraud and financial crime has been thoroughly erased by Wall Street's regulatory capture not only of the Federal Reserve and Treasury but of the Executive Branch of government itself.'

It is worth pointing out that there appears to be a revolving door between the big banks and the American Government with numerous individuals frequently moving to and fro without there apparently being any thought that this might be in some way compromising. Actually, of course, similar revolving doors connect the big American banks, particularly Goldman Sachs, and other Governments. The British Government has for some years appeared to be an outpost of Goldman Sachs.

The resulting depression which Obama created meant that the economy shrank and public sector budgets collapsed. Government at local, state and federal levels had to cut back social spending and cut pension commitment. In order to cut costs and raise money, government at all three levels sold public land and natural resources as well as basic infrastructure in order to pay back money owed to the banks. Interest rates fell to zero or thereabout for anyone who had savings but banks and credit card companies charged high interest rates with the average credit card owner paying 29% interest. Workers were squeezed by the rising cost of their debts. And after the junk mortgage crash, the Federal Reserve created trillions of dollars (out of nothing) to bail out the banks that had bad loans. The banks didn't use the money to help their customers but they used the money to give themselves huge bonuses to celebrate their failure.

The financial troubles that had started in America (thanks entirely to President Obama and the neoliberals) quickly spread around the world and in order to 'help' struggling countries, the IMF introduced austerity programmes. In countries everywhere, governments were given 'loans' and local taxpayers had to pay them back. Wages, living standards and currency values all fell. The American banks used the power of the dollar to ensure that they continued to make huge amounts of money.

2011

In 2011, the US, Britain and France launched a NATO attack on Libya. They captured, tortured and killed Colonel Gaddafi and then destroyed Libya. The country's gold reserves were stolen and the US Secretary of State, Hillary Clinton, gave Libya's arms to ISIS fighters so that they could attack Syria and Iraq. The aim was to prevent those countries from using their own oil to develop and grow stronger.

NATO attacked Libya because Colonel Gaddafi wanted to seek independence from America's control of Libyan oil. He wanted to use his country's oil to develop a proper educational system and a national social-welfare system. More dangerously for the US he wanted to create a gold backed African currency, throw out American military bases and obtain loans for construction from China instead of the World Bank. Libya had the highest standard of living in Africa and Gaddafi was sharing the revenue from oil sales with the country's citizens.

All that was more than enough to enrage the globalists who could see their power and influence waning and their control of the oil, and the money, disappearing.

And so Gaddafi was demonised and killed and his country 'captured', sacked and left in ruins. Today, thanks to America in general and Hillary Clinton in particular, Libya is a wild country where slaves are sold in open air markets.

2017

President Trump insisted in 2017, and then again in 2018, that the US had a right to take oil from Iraq and from Syria. The reason, he said, was that the oil would be payment for the cost of America having attacked those countries. In 2020, Tump repeated that America had the right to take the natural resources of any country that it attacked, as compensation for the cost of the attack – with absolutely no reparations.

America also attacked Venezuela, attempting (and failing) to depose President Maduro, and then persuading its NATO allies to impose sanctions on the country to disrupt the country's economy. When Venezuela wanted to use its gold to pay for food and medicine which the people needed, Britain (which was holding the country's reserves at the Bank of England and which had consistently sided with America in imposing sanctions on Venezuela) simply seized the gold and held it until the American government decided who to make President of the country. In a quite extraordinary judgement, a British high court judge said that it would be illegal to give Venezuela's gold to the elected President Maduro because the British Government didn't recognise him and wanted to make his political rival the President.

Much the same thing has happened almost everywhere in the world where there are supplies of oil, gas or valuable minerals. And it is these offensive actions, conducted by neoliberals fighting against democracy and freedom, which explain why America has been continuously at war since the 1940s and has attacked, interfered with or invaded over 200 countries since the end of the Second World War. Neoliberals see democratic laws as intruding on their liberty, and neoliberals do not believe in holding corporations liable for the damage that they cause. The trigger, of course, has often been oil and gas.

Today, oil and gas still remain vital for almost all human activities and America likes to keep control of the supply. And so, America put sanctions on European companies which were helping to build Russia's Nord Stream 2 gas pipeline. Germany offered to build port facilities to import US liquefied natural gas (at higher prices) but America still wasn't satisfied. The US was determined to stop the Nord Stream 2 pipeline and, therefore, to ensure that Europe had to buy American gas.

The war between Russia and Ukraine provided the US with a convenient opportunity to blow up the pipeline so that American oil and gas companies would once again control the supply of gas to Europe. The mainstream media claim that Russia blew up its own pipeline (when if it had wanted to stop the flow of gas all it had to do was turn off the tap) but it is generally understood outside the mainstream media that the Americans blew up the pipeline in order to preserve their own massively profitable sale of gas to European countries – even though this meant that European consumers had to pay vastly inflated prices for the heating, their fuel and, ultimately, their food. The high costs of fuel in Europe in 2022 and onwards were a direct result of American, not Russian, actions.

In the UK, the Government has punished its own electors by unilaterally imposing special taxes and conditions on oil and gas companies working the North Sea. This was allegedly done to help Britain reach net zero as quickly as possible.

The evidence shows conclusively that neoliberals run the world, which is now controlled by a new breed of individuals who have managed to meld communism and fascism with self-interest.

2018

It was in 2018 that a young Swedish girl called Greta Thunberg first began to attract publicity for her views on global warming. It seemed to me then (and seems even more so now) that she had simply been selected as a promotional tool by the conspirators. It is difficult for truth-tellers to attack a young girl (particularly one with a form of autism) who seems to believe in her message. And it is obviously difficult for critics to argue with a girl, however rude she might be, when she appears to have some sort of mental illness. For the conspirators, Greta also had the advantage of being quite small and unlikely to grow too tall too quickly. The one certainty in my mind is that Greta's rise to international fame didn't happen by accident or without a great deal of planning. Sadly, Greta Thunberg's claims have caused much needless anxiety and despair among children around the world.

A short book entitled *Greta's Homework* by Zina Cohen analyses and destroys the nonsense of climate change.

2020

The idea of the 15 minute city (or, as it is also called, the 20 minute city) first really came to global prominence in 2020 when the socialist mayor of Paris announced a plan to introduce the concept to the French capital.

The idea of the 15 minute city is that all daily necessities such as accommodation, food, shops, work, education, health care and leisure can be found within an area where everyone can get everywhere (on foot or by bicycle) within 15 minutes.

Within months, cities and towns all over the world were announcing that they would become 15 minute cities and that motorised traffic would be strictly controlled or even banned. Residents in 15 minute cities were told that they would only be allowed out of their area on a limited number of days a year. Road blocks, either manned or equipped with barriers would ensure that citizens obeyed the laws, and a plethora of CCTV cameras would help maintain discipline and ensure obedience.

It was claimed that the 15 (or 20) minute cities would help cut down travel and would, therefore, help deal with the imaginary threat of climate change.

According to a report from 'ARUP C40 Cities and University of Leeds' entitled *The Future of Urban Consumption*, the 'ambitious' target for the year 2030 is for individuals to eat no meat and no dairy produce and to have no household food waste. And the 'ambitious' target for the year 2030 is for each individual to purchase only three new clothing items per year. I wonder how many people realise that these targets have been proposed and what the consequences will be for industry (both manufacturing and retail). What about growing children and slimmers? Do they have to wait a year for a new pair of trousers? If you buy a shirt, a dress and a sock do you have to wait until the following year to buy the other sock?

Oh, and the plan is that there will no private vehicles whatsoever and individuals will be allowed one short-haul return flight (less than 1500 km) every three years. Laptops and similar electronic devices will be expected to last seven years. Good luck with that.

None of this proposal was decided democratically. None of this was put to the vote. I'd like to think that no one takes this stuff seriously but I know they do. This is the future that is planned for us.

2020-2023

Early in 2020, governments around the world claimed that humans everywhere were threatened by a new version of the plague. I dealt with this fake threat in a book called *Coming Apocalypse* which was published in April 2020 – just weeks after the fake scare had begun. (I dealt with the fake pandemic and its consequences in a series of books which are listed in the bibliography at the back of this book.)

During 2020, 2021 and 2022 and 2023, I repeatedly challenged the proponents of the covid-19 vaccine to debate the vaccine's qualities in public. I had published evidence warning that the so-called vaccine cold cause heart attacks, blood clots, myocarditis and immune system problems in the autumn of 2020 – before the vaccine roll out began. I explained that I would prove that the vaccine did not do what it was said to do, that it was incredibly dangerous and would be responsible for more deaths than would be saved.

Absurd figures were released suggesting that the covid-19 'vaccine' had saved millions of lives but no one ever attempted to provide any evidence to support this wild conjecture. I have been writing and broadcasting about vaccines probably longer than anyone alive but no one would debate with me. I am not surprised. Whenever it is considered inconvenient, which is most of the time, the truth must be suppressed and the truth-tellers must be oppressed and silenced.

Although they have never been shown to be safe nor effective, and what evidence is available shows that they do far more harm than good (my book *Anyone who tells you vaccines are safe and effective is lying: here's the proof* contains shocking statistical evidence about heavily promoted vaccines such as those for polio and smallpox) vaccination programmes are promoted heavily for a number of reasons: they can be used to force compliance, they make huge amounts of money for the pharmaceutical industry, they can be used to cull populations, they can be used to induce infertility in future generations and they enable governments to 'prove' that they are caring people, deeply concerned for the welfare of the public.

It is no exaggeration to say that, throughout the world, vaccination programmes have been 'weaponised'. Vaccines are not treatments, they are methods of control and destruction.

(As an aside, it is worth mentioning that vaccines, like other drugs, are often promoted on the basis of experiments performed on animals. However, such experiments are entirely worthless and are used because, not in spite of, the fact that they are misleading. There are two reasons why animal experiments should be abandoned. First, such experiments are notoriously unreliable and give misleading results more than they provide useful results. If you don't know which experiments are misleading then all experiments are worthless. Second, the drugs industry itself will dismiss unfavourable results on the basis that animals are so different to humans that tests done on animals are utterly unreliable. My book *Betrayal of Trust* contains the names and details of fifty pharmaceutical products which are known to cause serious problems when given to animals but which were approved for human use on the grounds that animal experiments are worthless. And yet new products, such as vaccines, are given approval at least partly on the basis that animal experiments were conducted.)

When the BBC in the UK founded a special unit called Verify to act as a sort of fact checking unit, I challenged the entire Verify Team to a live television debate about covid-19 and the covid-19 'vaccine'.

Naturally, I heard nothing.

Exactly the same thing that had happened in 2007-8, happened again in 2020-2022 during the fake covid pandemic.

The pattern has now become quite simple and straightforward. It is the same basic policy that the Americans used to destroy Russia (and help themselves to all the money) after the debacle of 1991.

As local economies are forced to collapse and fall into recession, politicians and bankers move in. Aided and abetted by the IMF and the World Bank, they offer loans at usurious interest rates and take over planning rules, land ownership and valuable resources.

The result of the 2020-2023 fake pandemic was that the American banks and financiers got much richer and the rest of the world (especially hard-working, decent people) got much poorer.

And, of course, the take-over of the world by the unscrupulous and greedy banking elite has spread into all areas of life.

So, for example, small farms and small businesses everywhere are being shut down permanently as government aid and support goes to the huge, often crooked international corporations who have hundreds of lobbyists and can afford to pay bribes to keep politicians happy. (When I say 'bribes' what I really mean, of course, is that large companies and bankers pay out huge sums in campaign contributions. And when politicians retire they invariably receive huge book advance payments that everyone knows will never be paid back out of royalties. Oh, and politicians are regularly paid vastly inflated fees for speaking engagements.)

During the fake covid pandemic of 2020 (I have used government figures to prove that the official claims were fake and these are available on my websites and in my videos) politicians in just about every country seemed to make the same 'mistakes' at almost exactly the same time – introducing lockdowns, mask wearing, social distancing and vaccination programmes which all did infinitely more harm than good. Politicians now claim that they were merely acting on 'best advice' and that if they made mistakes then the mistakes were made in good faith. But none of those things were mistakes. Despite the appearances nothing happened as a result of incompetence; everything happened by design. If politicians were merely incompetent it would be reasonable to assume that occasionally they would get things right: but they never do. Seemingly inexplicable and indefensible domestic and foreign policies in countries around the world were a result of careful planning, overseen by conspirators and put into action by enthusiastic, well-rewarded collaborators. It is absolutely no coincidence that every new government makes the same mistakes as its predecessors. And it is no accident that every new national and local government asks the people what they want and then ignores the answers.

2023

In 2023, the World Health Organisation made it clear that they plan to force everyone on earth to accept a barrage of vaccinations – to be jabbed with a whole sequence of jabs which don't do what they are supposed to do but which do kill people, make them infertile and create new illnesses.

The World Health Organisation's refreshed plan for global dominance via the needle was slipped out quietly while the mainstream media remains obsessed with the trivial activities of a bunch of Z list celebrities and minor royals and, occasionally, with the latest in a series of designer wars created by American conspirators and their friends in NATO.

There are people around who still don't realise this but the World Health Organisation is the terrorist wing of the United Nations, and for the last three years it has spread lies and fear with relentless enthusiasm. The WHO's job is to terrify the public and adapt the truth to suit the needs of the conspirators pushing for global power and a world government.

The WHO is an essential weapon in the UNs armoury. It has nothing whatsoever to do with health but is a plain and simple terrorist group and a vital part of the global conspiracy which is taking us remorselessly into the New World Order and dragging us down into the Great Reset.

The WHO is planning to bring a dangerous and unnecessary programme of compulsory vaccinations –all untested and dangerous. Disingenuous as always, they and their jack-booted collaborators will say, of course, that the vaccinations aren't compulsory and that if you don't want to buy food or electricity, have a bank account, keep a job or leave your home, you won't need a vaccination certificate. Of course if you do want to buy food and electricity, have a job, leave your home and generally stay alive then you'll need all your jabs but as the loathsome Trudeau would probably say they won't be compulsory.

They think we're all stupid and the tragedy is that they're nearly right: most people are stupid and most people will accept everything they're told by the WHO – an organisation now infamous for its links with the vaccine hobbyist Bill Gates – a man with close links with the cuddly trio of the BBC, *The Guardian* and Jeffrey Epstein.

In March 2020, over three years ago, I warned that they would introduce compulsory vaccinations. If you listen carefully you can still hear the sniggers and the abuse I received at the time. Totalitarian regimes have always introduced compulsory vaccination programmes – though they've never before been planned globally and they've always failed. I also warned about digital money and the rest of the plan.

Today, there is no need for any additional evidence proving that vaccines don't do what they are supposed to do and aren't safe. My book *Anyone who tells you vaccines are safe and effective is lying* is packed with information proving that vaccine programmes aren't safe or effective. And in the autumn of 2020, I recorded a series of free videos detailing exactly what problems the covid-19 jab would cause. I warned about the heart problems, the clots and the myocarditis months before those problems appeared and before the jabs roll out programme. Meanwhile, of course, mainstream media propaganda outfits were telling everyone that the vaccine was safe and effective.

The official figures prove that my warnings – the best part of three years ago – were absolutely accurate. The Government figures also show that there never was a pandemic and the remarketed over-promoted flu was just a pretty standard flu. The so-called vaccine, however, is one of the most toxic pharmaceutical products in history

– making thalidomide look good. The sensible folk who said NO to the toxic jab are today the healthiest people left on earth.

There is now no doubt the covid jab is a killer, fake vaccine – useless but far more dangerous than depleted uranium shells or cluster bombs. Like bombs, rockets and bullets its only conceivable purpose is to kill people.

The evidence showing that the over-promoted, over-sold covid-19 jab is the most dangerous pharmaceutical product ever used is denied only by fools or shills for the conspirators and the drug industry. I have repeatedly warned that the covid jab can and does cause or exacerbate a huge range of serious health problems – including heart disease, clotting problems and cancer. And as I warned two and a half years ago the immune system problems caused by the 'vaccine' are deadly.

The evidence suggesting that the covid vaccine is toxic is overwhelming and should be banned is constantly growing. Any other product known to cause such severe problems would have been taken off the market a long time ago.

A review of 325 autopsies on patients who died after covid vaccination showed that 74% of the deaths were caused by the covid vaccine. The nine eminent authors of the relevant medical paper found that the organ systems most likely to be involved in covid jab deaths were: cardiovascular system, haematological system and respiratory system. The mean time between vaccination to death was 14.3 days. A total of 240 deaths out of the 325 deaths were independently adjudicated as directly due to or significantly contributed to by covid-19 vaccinations.'

The nine authors concluded: 'The consistency seen among cases in this review with known covid-19 vaccine adverse effects, their mechanisms and related excess deaths, coupled with autopsy confirmation and physician-led death adjudication, suggests there is a high likelihood of causal link between covid-19 vaccines and death in most cases. Further urgent investigation is required for the purpose of clarifying our findings.'

Then there was the paper which appeared in the *British Journal of General Practice* recently which showed that 'enlargement of axillary, supraclavicular or cervical lymph nodes following vaccination with covid-19 mRNA vaccines is more frequent than initially reported, with a rate reaching up to 16% following the second dose of the Moderna mRNA vaccine.' The paper also reported that a few cases of lymphoma were reported in the literature.

The authors warned that doctors in charge of patients with post-vaccination lymphadenopathy should be reminded to consider the possibility of an underlying or coincidental malignant disorder.

The truth, of course, is that there aren't enough doctors around to check fully 16% of all the patients who have a second dose of that vaccine.

The covid jab is causing one problem after another. And the problems are ignored or suppressed by the medical establishment.

The covid-19 jab is responsible for a surge in type 1 diabetes among children and teenagers. A survey of 38,000 young people (reported in the *Journal of the American Medical Association*) showed that the rise is substantial. Over two years ago, I warned that this would happen. I warned that the covid-19 jab would push up blood sugar levels. The epidemic of type 1 diabetes is caused by the covid-19 vaccine. And the drug companies will now get ever richer selling treatments for diseases the drug companies caused.

Everywhere you look there is evidence proving that the covid jab was a killer. In less than two and a half years nearly 2,000 healthy athletes have had heart attacks or sudden serious health problems – with over 1,300 of them dying.

And yet the medical establishment, bought with drug company money, still refuses even to contemplate the idea that the deaths may be caused by their beloved vaccine. They daren't admit that the medical profession is responsible for thousands of unnecessary deaths because they're terrified of the inevitable lawsuits not to mention the professional embarrassment.

Doctors who gave the covid jab without properly assessing the dangers are going to be on the wrong end of the world's most expensive class action lawsuit.

But the vaccines have not been withdrawn. No one in the drug companies or the medical establishment is issuing grovelling apologies.

Instead, as has happened for over three years now, the doctors who are exposing the dangers of the covid-19 jab are being harassed, banned and censored.

Any doctor who still gives the covid-jab is a dangerous fool who should be struck off the medical register for life and arrested immediately for attempted murder.

Summary

Look back and it is clear that America has now been at war with the rest of the world for around 100 years. The designer or proxy war against Russia, taking place in Ukraine, followed, almost seamlessly, after the disastrous and damaging war in Afghanistan. which was a disaster to start with, a disaster throughout and a disaster at the end. Huge numbers of Afghans and Americans died for absolutely no reason and billions of dollars were wasted. As usual, no one has ever been sacked or held accountable.

It seems that for the Americans, or rather their political leaders, peace is now just a memory, not even available as an interlude between wars which have become a never-ending opportunity to spend more money on bombs, rockets and depleted uranium shells.

Since the end of World War II, America has created seemingly endless wars artificially based on race, ethnicity, gender, religion or a drive for 'democracy', but really about acquiring money, power and control of resources. America has become a pirate nation. (In the 1990s I wrote two books about American adventures. One was called *Rogue Nation* and the other was called *Global Bully*.) None of those wars was fought to defend American lives or property; all were fought to give the conspirators greater power and more money. All of those wars ended up costing Americans many lives and a great deal of money; all involved the transfer of money from citizens everywhere to the bank accounts and trust funds of the conspirators.

NATO and the CIA have been destabilising countries all over the world for more than half a century – paying for terrorist help whenever it has seemed useful and appropriate. They have, for example, destabilised much of Europe, with the result that atlases and history books are out of date almost before they are printed. One minute one leader in one country will be in favour and then, suddenly favours will move to another leader in another country. Groups of dissidents are encouraged, financed and armed if they promise to build a better financial relationship with America.

It was always inevitable that we would head straight for World War III, immediately after Russia was forced to invade Ukraine, previously described as one of the most corrupt countries on earth. Ukraine, remember, has persecuted Christians with a relentlessness that would have aroused screams of outrage a few years ago and has an army whose soldiers delight in wearing Nazi insignia.

America needs to attack and suppress both China and Russia. The conspirators have chosen to target Russia first but there is no doubt the militant conspirators in the United States plan to start a war with China.

We are being manipulated and controlled by a cabal of well-known politicians and billionaires and taken into a totalitarian society, with fear being the main driving force. The significance of fear in our lives can never be underestimated.

While writing this short book I was sitting in a café reading a volume of work by Petrarch and found these lines from Virgil in a piece by him entitled *The Ascent of Mount Ventoux*:

'Blessed the man who is skilled to understand
The hidden cause of things; who beneath his feet
All fear casts, and death's relentless doom,
And the howlings of greedy Acheron.'

If the real history of the 20th century and beyond is ever written (something which I am beginning to doubt) then Obama and the Clintons and their fellow neoliberals will be remembered as the world's most evil terrorists.

It is surprising, is it not, how many Presidents and Prime Ministers (such as Blair et al) began their terms of office with very little money in the bank, spent their years in office earning quite modest salaries (supported in the case of Biden with money paid into his account from Ukraine and China) and then, shortly after the conclusion of their term of office, become immensely rich.

The money paid to these former Presidents and Prime Ministers is usually handed over as massive advances for autobiographies that virtually no one will ever want to read or as extraordinarily high speaking fees for making speeches that virtually no one will ever want to listen to. The two Clintons were, between them, paid millions of dollars for their memoirs. When they were being investigated over corruption charges neither of them could remember anything.

The fees paid out to the conspirators and the collaborators are, of course, payments for services rendered while the individual was in office. And the main service rendered has been the creation of fear and the steady progress towards the Great Reset, the New World Order and a world government.

Part Four: Here's what you can do

The conspirators are taking us into the Great Reset through their control of the mainstream media and much of the internet – and they have an army of collaborators, bots and secret service operatives working on their behalf. In the UK, a special brigade of the British Army is employed in spreading misinformation and suppressing the truth. And GCHQ, the UK's spy agency, has been busy suppressing honest, science based comments on the internet if, for example, the authors of those comments ask questions about the covid-19 'vaccine'. Even qualified doctors with solid evidence to share have been suppressed and censored. I wonder how many of those soldiers and spies realise that they are working against their own country and their own countrymen and women – the very people who are paying their wages. In America both the CIA and the FBI have interfered with the freedom of truth-tellers to share vital information.

But there are more of us than there are of them and if we are to win then we have to do it by spreading the truth.

Please buy and give away copies of this book or lend your copy to others to read. Please don't worry that I'm doing this to get rich. Since early 2020 my reputation and income have been utterly destroyed and we have put most of our time into sharing the truth. The price of this book has been kept as low as we are allowed to make it. If we make any money from the sale of this book (which is unlikely) we will use it to buy more copies and spread them around.

The problem, of course, is that most people don't want to know the truth. They have been thoroughly brainwashed and they would rather just watch the TV soaps, play with their recycling boxes and find new apps to download onto their smart phones. But we need to persuade more people to open their eyes and to educate themselves in the interests of self-preservation. We need to have at least 5% of the population on our side if we are to survive, and everyone in that 5% needs to refuse to accept a digital currency or a digital passport and needs to refuse to carry a smart phone full of officially approved apps.

So, here's what you can do.

Buy copies of this book and give them to everyone you know. I have kept the royalty level as low as possible and I promise that, if I do earn anything from this book, every penny earned will be spent on buying and distributing copies to journalists, influencers, etc. (I have to buy copies from Amazon just like you do.)

Appendix 1: A short bibliography

I read hundreds of books, thousands of articles and watched a great many videos in the research, preparation and writing of this book. Below I have listed a few of the books I found most useful.

1984 by George Orwell
A Bigger Problem than Climate Change by Vernon Coleman
A cry from the Far Middle by P.J.O'Rourke
Agenda 21 by Ron Taylor
Animal Farm by George Orwell
BBC: Brainwashing Britain by David Sedgwick
Behind the Green Mask: UN Agenda 21 by Rosa Koire
Black water: The rise of the world's most powerful mercenary army by Jeremy Scahill
Blackwater: the rise of the world's most powerful mercenary army by Jeremy Scahill
Blind Eye to Murder by Tom Bower
Bloodless Revolution by Vernon Coleman
Brave New World by Aldous Huxley
Climategate, The Marijuana Conspiracy, Project Blue Beam by the Dot Connector Library
Coming Apocalypse by Vernon Coleman
Covid-19: Exposing the Lies by Vernon Coleman
Covid-19: The Fraud Continues by Vernon Coleman
Covid-19: The Greatest Hoax in History by Vernon Coleman
Dangerous Ideas by Eric Berkowitz
Destiny of Civilisation: Finance Capitalism, Industrial Capitalism or Socialism by Michael Hudson
Dirty Wars: The world is a battlefield by Jeremy Scahill
Dirty Wars: The world is a battlefield by Jeremy Scahill
Dynastic America and those who own it by Henry H Klein
Endgame by Vernon Coleman
Essays on Free Knowledge: The Origins of Wikipedia and the New Politics of Knowledge by Larry Sanger
Everything is Going to Get Worse by Vernon Coleman

Fifteen Decisive Battles of the World by Sir Edward Creasy
Fog Facts by Larry Beinhart
Greta's Homework by Zina Cohen
Hidden Dangers: How governments, telecom and electric power utilities suppress the truth about the known hazards of electromagnetic field (EMF) radiation by Captain Jerry G.Flynn
Hidden Persuaders by Vance Packard
Illuminati Agenda 21 by Dean and Jill Henderson
Living in a Fascist Country by Vernon Coleman
Love among the Ruins by Evelyn Waugh
Nobody Knows Anything by Robert Moriarty
None Dare Call it Conspiracy by Gary Allen with Larry Abraham
Notes on Nationalism by George Orwell
OFPIS by Vernon Coleman
Orwell on Truth by George Orwell
Parliament of Whores by P.J.O'Rourke
Politics and the English Language by George Orwell
Powershift by Alvin Toffler
Presstitutes: Embedded in the Pay of the CIA by Udo Ulfkotte
Say NO to the New World Order by Gary Allen
Science, Liberty and Peace by Aldous Huxley
Scrap the BBC by Richard D.North
Shaping the Future of the Fourth Industrial Revolution: A Guide to Building a Better World by Klaus Schwab
Social Media: Nightmare on Your Street by Vernon Coleman
Sold Out by James Richards
Stuffed! By Vernon Coleman
Technocracy: The Hard Road to World Order by Patrick M.Wood
The Art of War by Sun Tzu
The Collapse of Antiquity by Michael Hudson
The Creature from Jekyll Island: A Second Look at the Federal Reserve by G.Edward Griffin
The Dark Side of Camelot – Seymour Hersh
The Death of Money by James Rickards
The Fourth and Richest Reich by Edwin Hartrich
The Globalisation of Poverty and the New World Order by Michel Chossudovsky
The Greening by Larry Abraham
The Greening of America by Charles A.Reick

The Hidden Enemy: The German Threazt to Post-War Peace by Heinz Pol

The Lessons of History by Will and Ariel Durant

The Limits of State Action by Wilhelm von Humboldt

The Man Versus the State by Herbert Spencer

The New Germany and the Old Nazis byT.H.Tetens

The Octopus: Europe in the grip of organised crime by Brian Freemantle

The Press by A.J.Liebling

The Revolt of the Masses by Jose Ortega y Gasset

The Rockefeller File by Gary Allen

The Shocking History of the EU by Zina Cohen

The Social Contract by Rousseau

The Social Credit System in China by Anonymous

The Tainted Source: The Undemocratic Origins of the European Idea by John Laughland

The Tycoons: How Andrew Carnegie, John D Rockefeller, Jay Gould and J.P.Morgan invented the American supereconomy by Charles R Morris

They want your money and your life by Vernon Coleman

Tower of Basel: The Shadowy History of the Secret Bank that Runs the World by Adam Lebor

Trading with the Enemy by Charles Higham

Tragedy & Hope by Carroll Quigley

Unmasked: Inside Antifa's Radical Plan to Destroy Democracy by Andy Ngo

US-Imposed Post 9/11Muslim Holocaust and Muslim Genocide by Gideon Maxwell Polya

Appendix 2: Author biography

Sunday Times bestselling author Vernon Coleman qualified as a doctor in 1970 and has worked both in hospitals and as a principal in general practice. Vernon Coleman is a multi-million selling author and since 1975, he has written over 100 books which have sold over three million copies in the UK, been in bestseller lists around the world and been translated into 26 languages. Several of his books have been on the bestseller lists and in the UK paperback editions of his books have been published by Pan, Penguin, Corgi, Arrow, Century, RKP, Mandarin and Star among many others. His books have been adapted for television, radio and the cinema and serialised in newspapers around the world and his novel 'Mrs Caldicot's Cabbage War' was turned into a successful, award winning movie. He has appeared on Top Gear (the motoring programme), written for a DIY magazine and contributed to a cookery video. He has presented numerous programmes on television and radio, including several series based on his best-selling book Bodypower which was voted one of the 100 most popular books by British readers.

Vernon Coleman has written columns for the Daily Star, Sun, Sunday Express, Planet on Sunday and The People (resigning from the latter when the editor refused to publish a column questioning the morality and legality of invading Iraq) and many other publications and has contributed over 5,000 articles, columns and reviews to 100 leading British publications including Daily Telegraph, Sunday Telegraph, Guardian, Observer, Sunday Times, Daily Mail, Mail on Sunday, Daily Express, Woman, Woman's Own, Punch and Spectator. His columns and articles have also appeared in hundreds of leading magazines and newspapers throughout the rest of the world. He edited the British Clinical Journal and the European Medical Journal and for twenty years he wrote a column which was syndicated to over 40 leading regional newspapers in the UK and to papers all around the world. Local health officials were often so irritated by the column that they paid doctors to write competing columns without charge. Fortunately, with a few exceptions, this made little difference to the success of the column.

In the UK, Vernon Coleman was the TV AM doctor on breakfast TV and when he commented that fatty food had killed more people than Hitler, he wasn't fired until several weeks after a large food lobbyist had threatened to pull all its advertising. He was the first networked television Agony Aunt, working on the BBC. Many millions consulted his Telephone Doctor advice lines and for six years he wrote a monthly newsletter which had subscribers in 17 countries.

In recent years Vernon has been banned from all mainstream media because his views are often at variance with those of the medical establishment. Since March 2020, the ban has been extended to include most of the internet and he is currently banned using or even accessing YouTube because the videos he made contained uncomfortable truths. He made over 300 videos which have all been censored or banned. He was refused admittance to Facebook, being told that he would be 'a threat to the Facebook community', expelled from LinkedIn (with no reason given) and banned from all social media. For over 30 years he has had a website (www.vernoncoleman.com) and right from the start the site has been visited regularly by representatives of the CIA, the FBI and by members of armed forces around the world.

Vernon Coleman has a medical degree, and an honorary science doctorate. He has worked for the Open University in the UK and was an honorary Professor of Holistic Medical Sciences at the Open International University based in Sri Lanka. He worked as a general practitioner for ten years (resigning from the NHS after being fined for refusing to divulge confidential information about his patients to State bureaucrats) and has organised numerous campaigns both for people and for animals. He can ride a bicycle and swim, though not at the same time. He likes animals, cricket (before they started painting slogans on the grass), cycling, cafés and collecting cigarette cards. Vernon Coleman is a bibliophile and has a library larger than most towns. He used to enjoy cricket when it was played as a sport by gentlemen and loves log fires and making bonfires.

Since 1999 he has been very happily married to the professional artist and author, Donna Antoinette Coleman to whom he is devoted and with whom he has co-written five books. They live in the delightful if isolated village of Bilbury in Devon where they have designed for themselves a unique world to sustain and nourish them in these dark and difficult times. They rarely leave home.

Appendix 3: What the papers say:

'Vernon Coleman writes as a general practitioner who has become disquieted by the all-pervasive influence of the pharmaceutical industry in modern medicine...He describes, with a wealth of illustrations, the phenomena of modern iatrogenesis; but he is also concerned about the wider harm which can result from doctors' and patients' preoccupation with medication instead of with the prevention of disease. He demonstrates, all the more effectively because he writes in a sober, matter-of-fact style, the immense influence exercised by the drug industry on doctors' prescribing habits...He writes as a family doctor who is keenly aware of the social dimensions of medical practice. He ends his book with practical suggestions as to how medical care – in the developing countries as well as in the West – can best be freed from this unhealthy pharmaceutical predominance.' – G.M.Carstairs, The Times Literary Supplement (1975)

'What he says of the present is true: and it is the great merit of the book that he says it from the viewpoint of a practising general practitioner, who sees from the inside what is going on, and is appalled by the consequences to the profession, and to the public.' – Brian Inglis, Punch (1975)

'Dr Coleman writes with more sense than bias. Required reading for any Minister of Health' – Daily Express

'I hope this book becomes a bestseller among doctors, nurses and the wider public...' – Nursing Times

'Dr Coleman's well-coordinated book could not be more timely.' – Yorkshire Post

'Few would disagree with Dr Coleman that more should be done about prevention.' – The Lancet

'This short but very readable book has a message that is timely. Vernon Coleman's point is that much of the medical research into which money and expertise are poured is useless. At the same time, remedial conditions of mind and body which cause the most distress are largely neglected. This is true.' – Daily Telegraph

'If you believe Dr Vernon Coleman, the main beneficiaries of the hundred million pounds worth of research done in this country each year are certainly not the patients. The research benefits mostly the medical place seekers, who use their academic investigations as rungs on the promotional ladder, or drug companies with an eye for the latest market opening...The future may hold bionic superman but all a nation's physic cannot significantly change the basic mortality statistics except sometimes, to make them worse.' – The Guardian

'Dr Coleman's well-coordinated book could not be more timely.' – Yorkshire Post

'The Medicine Men is well worth reading' – Times Educational Supplement

'Dr Vernon Coleman...is not a mine of information – he is a fountain. It pours out of him, mixed with opinions which have an attractive common sense ring about them.' – Coventry Evening Telegraph

'When the children have finished playing the games on your Sinclair or Commodore Vic 20 computer, you can turn it to more practical purposes. For what is probably Britain's first home doctor programme for computers is now available. Dr Vernon Coleman, one of the country's leading medical authors, has prepared the text for a remarkable series of six cassettes called The Home Doctor Series. Dr Coleman, author of the new book 'Bodypower'...has turned his attention to computers.' – The Times 1983

'The Medicine Men' by Dr Vernon Coleman, was the subject of a 14 minute 'commercial' on the BBC's Nationwide television programme recently. Industry doctors and general practitioners come in for a severe drubbing: two down and several more to go because the targets for Dr Coleman's pen are many, varied and, to say the least, surprising. Take the physicians who carry out clinical trials: many of those, claims the author, have sold themselves to the industry and agreed to do research for rewards of one kind or another, whether that reward be a trip abroad, a piece of equipment, a few dinners, a series of published papers or simply money.' – The Pharmaceutical Journal

'By the year 2020 there will be a holocaust, not caused by a plutonium plume but by greed, medical ambition and political opportunism. This is the latest vision of Vernon Coleman, an articulate and prolific medical author…this disturbing book detects diseases in the whole way we deliver health care.' – Sunday Times (1988)

'…the issues explores he explores are central to the health of the nation.' – Nursing Times

'It is not necessary to accept his conclusion to be able to savour his decidedly trenchant comments on today's medicine…a book to stimulate and to make one argue.' – British Medical Journal

'As a writer of medical bestsellers, Dr Vernon Coleman's aim is to shock us out of our complacency…it's impossible not to be impressed by some of his arguments.' – Western Daily Press

'Controversial and devastating' – Publishing News

'Dr Coleman produces mountains of evidence to justify his outrageous claims.' – Edinburgh Evening News

'Dr Coleman lays about him with an uncompromising verbal scalpel, dipped in vitriol, against all sorts of sacred medical cows.' – Exeter Express and Echo

'Vernon Coleman writes brilliant books.' – The Good Book Guide

'No thinking person can ignore him. This is why he has been for over 20 years one of the world's leading advocates on human and animal rights in relation to health. Long may it continue.' – The Ecologist

'The calmest voice of reason comes from Dr Vernon Coleman.' – The Observer

'A godsend.' – Daily Telegraph

'Dr Vernon Coleman has justifiably acquired a reputation for being controversial, iconoclastic and influential.' – General Practitioner

'Superstar.' – Independent on Sunday

'Brilliant!' – The People

'Compulsive reading.' – The Guardian

'His message is important.' – The Economist

'He's the Lone Ranger, Robin Hood and the Equalizer rolled into one.' – Glasgow Evening Times

'The man is a national treasure.' – What Doctors Don't Tell You

'His advice is optimistic and enthusiastic.' – British Medical Journal

'Revered guru of medicine.' – Nursing Times

'Gentle, kind and caring' – Western Daily Press

'His trademark is that he doesn't mince words. Far funnier than the usual tone of soupy piety you get from his colleagues.' – The Guardian

'Dr Coleman is one of our most enlightened, trenchant and sensitive dispensers of medical advice.' – The Observer

'Vernon Coleman is a leading medical authority and known to millions through his writing, broadcasting and bestselling books.' –

Woman's Own

'His book Bodypower is one of the most sensible treatises on personal survival that has ever been published.' – Yorkshire Evening Post

'One of the country's top health experts.' – Woman's Journal

'Dr Coleman is crusading for a more complete awareness of what is good and bad for our bodies. In the course of that he has made many friends and some powerful enemies.' – Western Morning News

'Brilliant.' – The People

'Dr Vernon Coleman is one of our most enlightened, trenchant and sensible dispensers of medical advice.' – The Observer

'The most influential medical writer in Britain. There can be little doubt that Vernon Coleman is the people's doctor.' – Devon Life

'The medical expert you can't ignore.' – Sunday Independent

'A literary genius.' – HSL Newsletter

'I would much rather spend an evening in his company than be trapped for five minutes in a radio commentary box with Mr Geoffrey Boycott.' – Peter Tinniswood, Punch

'Hard hitting...inimitably forthright.' – Hull Daily Mail

'Refreshingly forthright.' – Liverpool Daily Post

'Outspoken and alert.' – Sunday Express

'The man with a mission.' – Morning News

'A good read...very funny and packed with interesting and useful advice.' –The Big Issue

'Dr Coleman gains in stature with successive books' – Coventry Evening Telegraph

'Dr Coleman made me think again.' – BBC World Service

'Marvellously succinct, refreshingly sensible.' – The Spectator

'The living terror of the British medical establishment. A doctor of science as well as a medical graduate. Dr Coleman is probably one of the most brilliant men alive today. His extensive medical knowledge renders him fearless.' – Irish Times

'His future as King of the media docs is assured.' – The Independent

'Britain's leading medical author.' – The Star

'His advice is practical and readable.' – Northern Echo

'The layman's champion.' –Evening Herald

'All commonsense and no nonsense.' – Health Services Management

'One of Britain's leading experts.' – Slimmer Magazine

'The only three things I always read before the programme are Andrew Rawnsley in the Observer, Peter Hitchens in the Mail and Dr Vernon Coleman in The People. Or, if I'm really up against it, just Vernon Coleman.' – Eddie Mair, Presenter on BBC's Radio Four

'Dr Coleman is more illuminating than the proverbial lady with the lamp' – Company Magazine

'Britain's leading health care campaigner.' – The Sun

'What he says is true.' – Punch

'Perhaps the best known health writer for the general public in the world today.' – The Therapist

'The patient's champion. The doctor with the common touch.' – Birmingham Post

'A persuasive writer whose arguments, based on research and experience, are sound.' – Nursing Standard

'Coleman is controversial but respected and has been described in the British press as `the sharpest mind in medial journalism' and `the calmest voice of reason'. – Animals Today

'Vernon Coleman...rebel with a cause.' – Belfast Newsletter

'...presents the arguments against drug based medicine so well, and disturbs a harmful complacency so entertainingly.' – Alternative News

'He is certainly someone whose views are impossible to ignore, with his passionate advocacy of human and animal rights.' – International Journal of Alternative and Complementary Medicine

'The doctor who dares to speak his mind.' – Oxford Mail

'Dr Coleman speaks openly and reassuringly.' – Oxford Times

'He writes lucidly and wittily.' – Good Housekeeping

Appendix 4: Reference Articles referring to Vernon Coleman (Included to counter some of the lies on the internet)

Ref 1

'Volunteer for Kirkby' – The Guardian, 14.5.1965

Ref 2

'Bumbledom forced me to leave the NHS' – Pulse, 28.11.1981

Ref 3

'I'm Addicted To The Star' – The Star, 10.3.1988

Ref 4

'Medicine Becomes Computerised: Plug In Your Doctor.' – The Times, 29.3.1983

Ref 5

'Computer aided decision making in medicine' – British Medical Journal, 8.9.1984 and 27.10.1984

Ref 6

'Conscientious Objectors' – Financial Times magazine, 9.8.2003

Ref 7

'Doctor with the Common Touch.' – Birmingham Post, 9.10.1984

Ref 8

'Sacred Cows Beware: Vernon Coleman publishing again.' – The Scotsman, 6.12.1984

Ref 9

'Our Doctor Coleman Is Mustard' – The Sun, 29.6.1988

Ref 10

'Reading the mind between the lines.' – BMA News Review, November 1991

Ref 11

Doctors' Firsts – BMA News Review, 21.2.1996

Ref 12

'The big league of self publishing.' – Daily Telegraph, 17.8.1996

Ref 13

'Doctoring the books' – Independent, 16.3.1999

Ref 14

'Sick Practices' – Ode Magazine, July/August 2003

Ref 15

'You have been warned, Mr Blair.' – Spectator, 6.3.2004 and 20.3.2004
Ref 16
'Food for thought with a real live Maverick.' – Western Daily Press, 5.9.2006
Ref 17
'The doctor will see you now' – Independent, 14.5.2008

There is a more comprehensive list of reference articles on www.vernoncoleman.com

Final Note from the Author:
If you found this book informative I would be very grateful if you would put a suitable review online. It helps more than you can imagine. If you disliked the book, or disapproved of it in any way, please forget you read it.
Vernon Coleman

Printed in Great Britain
by Amazon

42722553R00106